Macbook

For Seniors

A Simple Step By Step Guide For Beginners

Jason Brown

Table of Contents

SETTING UP YOUR MACBOOK

Turn on your Macbook and get started!
Set up your new Mac in a few simple steps.

HARDWARE & SOFTWARE OVERVIEW FOR ALL MODELS

MACBOOK AIR

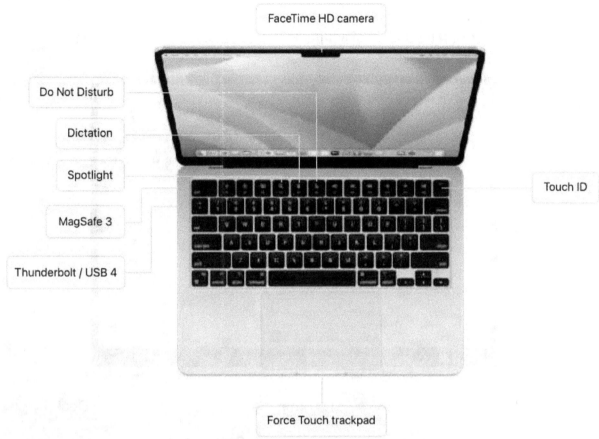

FaceTime HD camera

Do Not Disturb

Dictation

Spotlight

MagSafe 3

Thunderbolt / USB 4

Touch ID

Force Touch trackpad

MACBOOK PRO 13"+

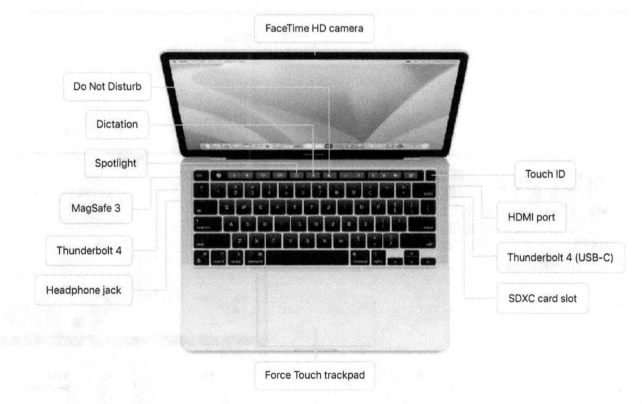

FaceTime HD camera

Do Not Disturb

Dictation

Spotlight

MagSafe 3

Thunderbolt 4

Headphone jack

Touch ID

HDMI port

Thunderbolt 4 (USB-C)

SDXC card slot

Force Touch trackpad

SOFTWARE OVERVIEW FOR ALL MODELS

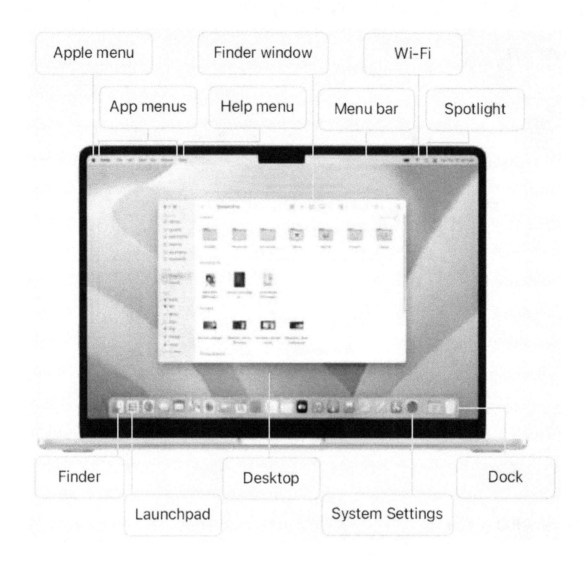

Apple menu   Finder window   Wi-Fi

App menus   Help menu   Menu bar   Spotlight

Finder   Desktop   Dock

Launchpad   System Settings

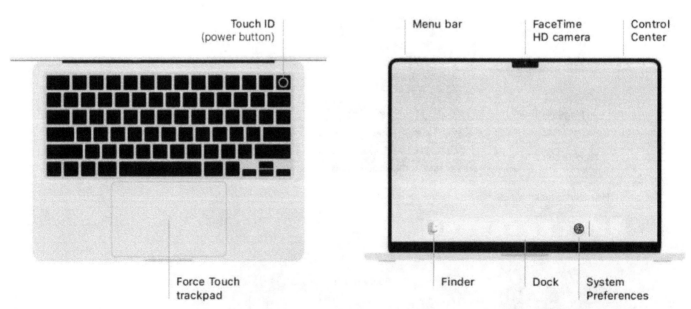

Touch ID
(power button)

Menu bar   FaceTime
HD camera   Control
Center

Force Touch
trackpad

Finder   Dock   System
Preferences

POWER-UP YOUR MACBOOK

To power up your MacBook, follow these straightforward steps:

1. Locate the Power Button: On most MacBook models, the power button is located at the top-right corner of the keyboard.
2. Press the Power Button: Gently press the power button. You should hear a startup chime (on older MacBooks) or see the screen illuminate.
3. Wait for Startup: Your MacBook will boot up, and you'll see the Apple logo on the screen. Depending on your MacBook's model and configuration, this process may take a few moments.
4. Log In: Once your MacBook has started up, you'll be prompted to log in with your username and password, if you have set up a password. Follow the on-screen instructions to do so.
5. You're Ready to Go: After successfully logging in, you'll be taken to your desktop, and your MacBook is now powered up and ready for use.

Remember to shut down your MacBook properly when you're done using it. To do this, click on the Apple menu in the top-left corner and choose "Shut Down." This ensures that your MacBook closes all programs and processes safely.

Charge with MagSafe 3

1. Plug the USB-C power adaptor into a plug socket.
2. Plug the USB-C end of the MagSafe 3 cable into the power adaptor.
3. Connect the other end of the cable to the MagSafe 3 port on your Mac.

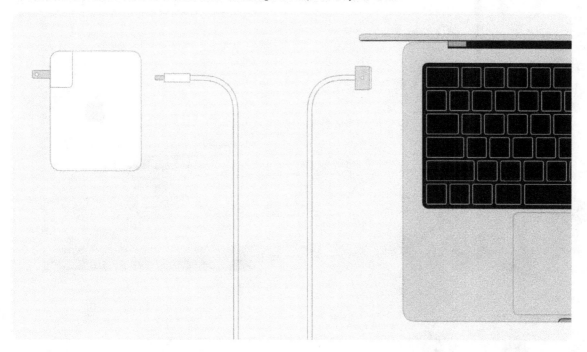

CHARGING YOUR MACBOOK

To charge your MacBook Air or MacBook Pro, follow these steps based on the type of port your Mac laptop has:

MAGSAFE 3 PORT

1. Locate the MagSafe 3 port on your Mac. It's typically found on the far left-hand side of the computer, near the escape key.

2. Charge with MagSafe 3:
   - Plug the USB-C power adaptor into a plug socket.
   - Connect the USB-C end of the MagSafe 3 cable to the power adaptor.
   - Attach the other end of the cable to the MagSafe 3 port on your Mac.

3. After connecting the charger, check the indicator light. It will glow green if your battery is fully charged or amber if your battery is charging or charging is on hold.

Note: MagSafe 3 charging is available for these Mac laptops:
   - MacBook Air introduced in 2022 or later
   - 14-inch MacBook Pro introduced in 2021 or later
   - 16-inch MacBook Pro introduced in 2021 or later

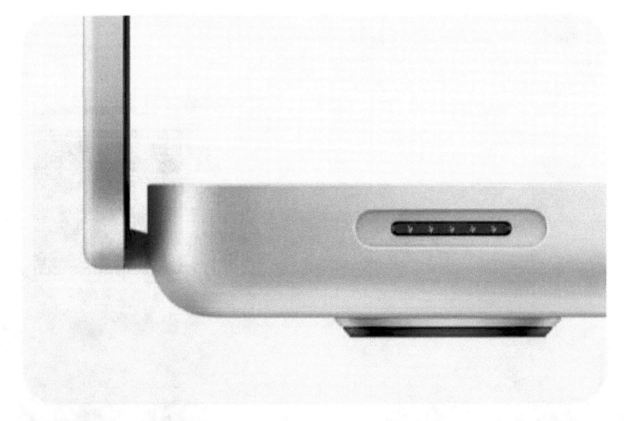

USB-C PORT

1. Locate the USB-C ports on your Mac. These ports can be found on the left-hand side or both sides of the computer.

2. Charge with USB-C
   2. Plug the power adaptor into a plug socket.
   3. Connect one end of the USB-C cable to the power adaptor.
   4. Plug the other end of the cable into any USB-C port on your Mac.

Note: USB-C charging is available for these Mac laptops:
- MacBook Pro introduced in 2016 or later
- MacBook Air introduced in 2018 or later
- MacBook introduced in 2015 or later
- Your Mac can only charge through one port at a time, so connecting multiple power adaptors to both USB-C ports and the MagSafe 3 port (if available) won't speed up charging.
- Different USB-C charge cables support varying maximum wattages (W). Ensure you use a cable that matches your Mac's requirements.
- If your display, such as the Apple Studio Display, provides power to your Mac, you don't need a separate USB-C power adaptor.

If the indicator light on your MagSafe 3 connector flashes amber repeatedly, try the provided troubleshooting steps. If the issue persists, contact Apple for further assistance.

GET STARTED WITH YOUR MAC

Setting up your MacBook is a straightforward process that involves several important steps. Here's a breakdown of what you'll be guided through during the initial setup:

1. Set Your Country or Region:
   • This step helps determine the language and time zone for your Mac.

2. Accessibility Options:
   • You have the option to explore accessibility features for Vision, Motor, Hearing, and Cognitive abilities. If not needed immediately, you can choose "Not Now."

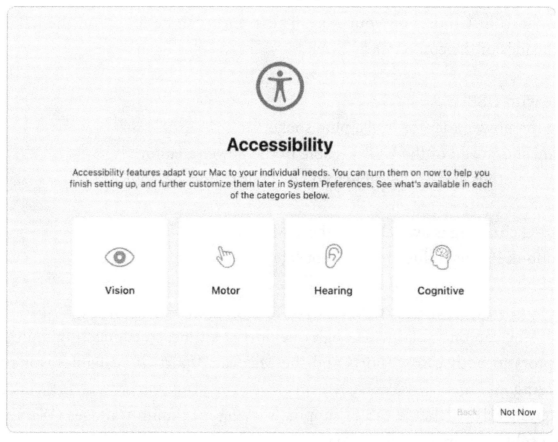

3. Connect to a Wi-Fi Network:
   • Select a Wi-Fi network and enter its password, if required. If you're using an Ethernet connection, you can choose "Other Network Options." You can also change the network settings later by clicking the Wi-Fi status icon 📶 in the menu bar or going to System Preferences > Wi-Fi.

4. Transfer Information (Optional):
   - If you want to transfer data from another computer, you can do so now or at a later time. If setting up a new computer without a previous Mac, you can choose "Not Now."

5. Sign in with Your Apple ID:
   - Your Apple ID is crucial for various Apple services. If you don't have one, you can create it during setup. Using the same Apple ID across your devices ensures seamless integration.

6. Store Files in iCloud (Optional):
   - iCloud allows you to store and access your content from anywhere. You can set this up later in System Settings.

7. Screen Time:
   - This feature allows you to monitor and receive reports on your computer usage. Details can be found in the Screen Time settings.

8. Enable Siri and "Hey Siri":
   - You can activate Siri and "Hey Siri" voice commands during setup. Instructions will be provided.

9. Set Up Touch ID:
   - If your MacBook Pro supports Touch ID, you can add your fingerprint during setup. To configure Touch ID later or add more fingerprints, go to System Settings > Touch ID & Password. To add a fingerprint, click the ➕ button and follow the onscreen instructions. You can use Touch ID for various purposes, such as unlocking your Mac and making purchases.

10. Set Up Apple Pay (Optional):
    - You have the option to set up Apple Pay for one user account. Additional users can use Apple Pay with their iPhone or Apple Watch.

11. Choose Your Desktop Appearance:
    - You can select between Light, Dark, or Auto mode for your desktop appearance. This choice can be adjusted later in System Settings.

Throughout this process, you have the flexibility to skip certain steps and complete them at a later time. Following these steps will ensure your MacBook Pro is set up according to your preferences and needs.

APPLE ID ON MAC

Your Apple ID is a crucial account that grants access to a range of Apple services. You can utilize it to download apps from the App Store, access media in Apple Music, Apple Podcasts, Apple TV, and Apple Books, synchronize content across devices using iCloud, create a Family Sharing group, and much more.

Manage family members, parental controls, purchases, and more.

Update account information.

Turn iCloud on or off.

Manage media accounts.

See all devices signed in with your Apple ID.

Here are some important details about managing your Apple ID:

1. Forgotten Password:
   • If you forget your Apple ID password, there's no need to create a new one. Simply

click "Forgot Apple ID or password?" in the sign-in window to retrieve your password.

2. Family Members:
   - Each family member using Apple devices should have their own Apple ID. You can create Apple ID accounts for your children and share purchases and subscriptions with Family Sharing.

3. Accessing Apple ID Settings:
   - Manage everything related to your Apple ID in System Settings on your MacBook. Your Apple ID and Family Sharing settings can be found at the top of the sidebar. To sign in with your Apple ID, if you haven't already, click "Sign in with your Apple ID" at the top of the sidebar.

4. Update Account Information:
   - In System Settings, click your Apple ID in the sidebar. Here, you can review and update the information associated with your account, including your name, contact information, and email subscriptions.

5. Password & Security:
   - Change your Apple ID password, enable two-factor authentication, manage trusted phone numbers, and generate verification codes. You can also control which apps and websites use Sign in with Apple.

6. Payment & Shipping:
   - Manage your payment methods and shipping address for Apple Store purchases.

7. iCloud:
   - Customize which iCloud features you want to enable or disable. When you activate an iCloud feature, your content is stored in iCloud, allowing you to access it across devices signed in with the same Apple ID.

8. Media & Purchases:
   - Manage accounts linked to Apple Music, Apple Podcasts, Apple TV, and Apple Books. Adjust purchasing settings and handle subscriptions.

9. Devices Associated with Your Apple ID:

- View all the devices linked to your Apple ID. Verify that Find My [device] is activated for each one. You can also check the status of iCloud Backup for iOS or iPadOS devices and remove devices you no longer own.

10. Family Sharing:
- Set up a family group for up to six members. This allows you to share and manage purchases, share device locations, and mark devices as lost in Find My. You can also supervise how your children use their devices and set Screen Time limits.

11. Account Recovery and Legacy Contact:
- Establish recovery contacts or set up a recovery key to assist in resetting your password and regaining access to your account. Additionally, designate trusted individuals as Legacy Contacts to access your account and personal information after your passing.

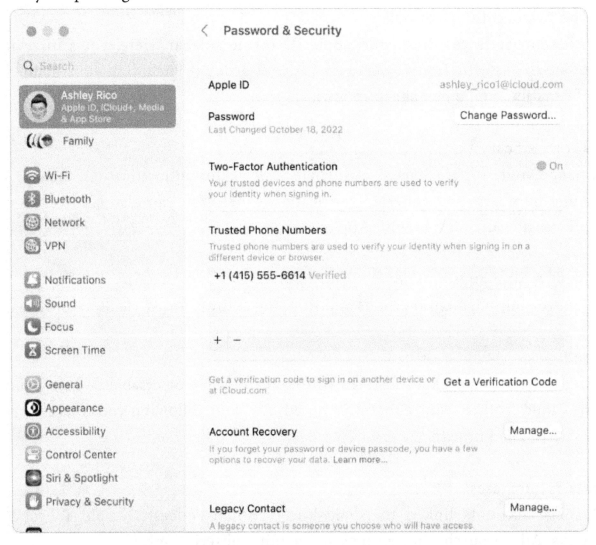

Your Apple ID is a versatile tool that enables seamless access to a variety of Apple services and allows you to manage your digital life efficiently.

CUSTOMIZE YOUR DESKTOP TO SUIT YOUR PREFERENCES

You have the option to select a basic color, use a favorite image, or even set a scenic photo that transitions with the time of day.

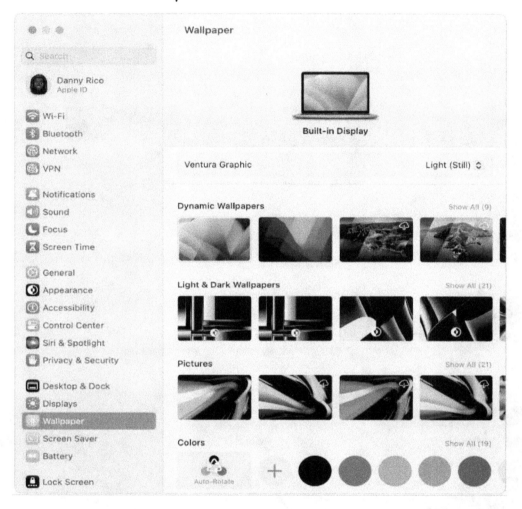

On your Mac, follow these steps to personalize your desktop:

1. Click on the Apple menu located in the top-left corner of your screen.
2. Choose "System Preferences" from the menu.
3. In the System Preferences window, find and click on Wallpaper in the sidebar. You may need to scroll down to see it.

LIGHT OR DAY

You can customize the appearance of your Mac by choosing between light, dark, or an automatic appearance that adapts based on the time of day.

Choose the color scheme for your Mac.

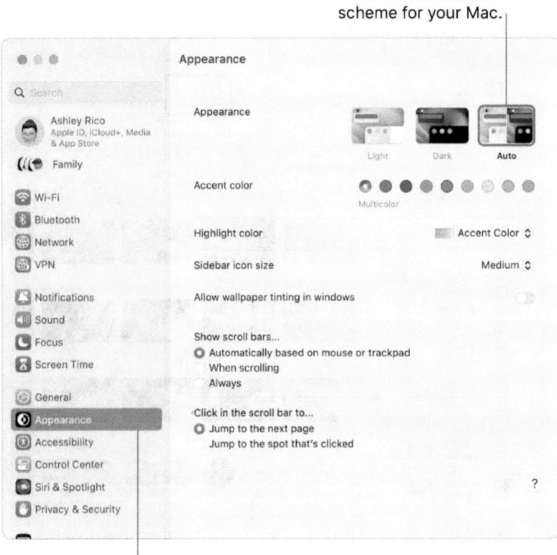

Click an item in the sidebar to adjust settings.

1. Open System Preferences
- Click the Apple menu in the top-left corner of your screen.
- Select "System Preferences" from the dropdown menu.

2. Access Appearance Settings
- In the System Preferences window, find and click on the "Appearance" icon .

3. Choose Your Appearance

- In the Appearance settings, you have three options:
  - Light: This provides a light appearance that remains constant.
  - Dark: This provides a dark appearance that remains constant. Dark Mode is especially useful for tasks like viewing documents, presentations, photos, movies, and web pages.

Auto:

This automatically switches between light and dark appearances based on your Night Shift schedule, which you can set separately. Auto won't switch the appearance until your Mac has been idle for at least a minute or if an app is preventing the display from sleeping, such as during media playback.

4. Customize Accent and Highlight Colors (Optional)
- In the same Appearance settings, you can also choose an accent color for buttons, pop-up menus, and other user interface (UI) controls.
- You can select a highlight color to use for highlighting selected text.

5. Dynamic Desktop Images
- Note that some dynamic desktop pictures may provide still images to ensure they don't distract from the selected light or dark appearance. For example, if you chose the dark appearance during macOS setup, the desktop picture will be set to a dark still image.
- You can change your desktop picture by following the "Change Wallpaper settings" option.

6. Quick Access to Dark Mode
- You can quickly toggle Dark Mode on or off through Control Centre . Click the Control Centre icon in the menu bar, then click "Display," and finally, click "Dark Mode."

DESKTOP, MENU BAR, AND HELP ON YOUR MAC

The desktop is the first thing you see on your MacBook. It's where you can access apps, search for items on your Mac and the web, organize your files, and more.

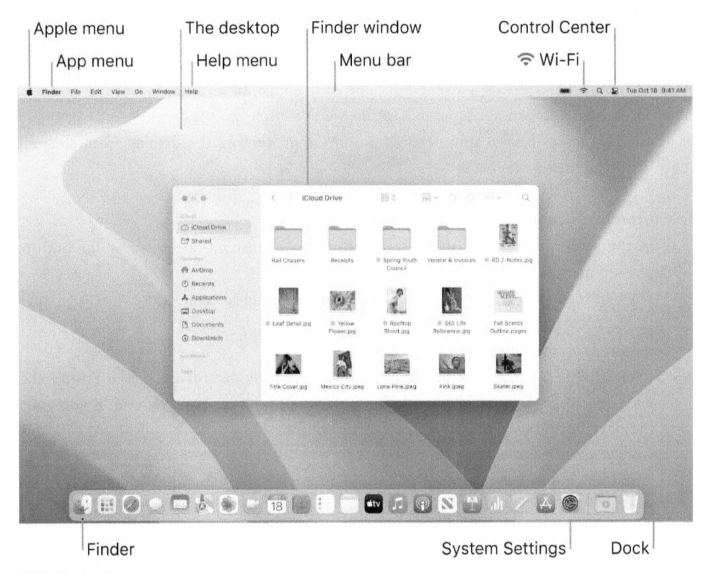

MENU BAR

- The menu bar is located at the top of the screen. It provides access to various commands and tasks within apps. The options in the menus change depending on the app you're using. On the right side of the menu bar, you'll find icons for tasks like connecting to Wi-Fi 📶 checking battery status 🔋 accessing Control Center ⚙, and using Spotlight search 🔍.

APPLE MENU

- The Apple menu found in the upper-left corner of the screen, contains frequently used items. Clicking the Apple icon opens this menu.

APP MENU

- You can have multiple apps and windows open simultaneously. The name of the active app appears in bold to the right of the Apple menu . The app's unique menus are listed below. When you switch to a different app or window, the app menu and the menus in the menu bar adjust accordingly.

HELP MENU

- Help for your MacBook is always accessible in the menu bar. To access it, open the Finder in the Dock, click the Help menu, and select "macOS Help" to open the macOS User Guide. You can also type in the search field for suggestions. For app-specific help, open the app and click "Help" in the menu bar.

ORGANIZING WITH STACKS

- You can group files on your desktop into stacks to maintain organization. Stacks can be arranged by type, date, or tag, helping keep your desktop tidy. Clicking a stack expands its contents, and hovering over it shows thumbnail images of the files. To create stacks, click the desktop and select "View > Use Stacks." You can also set grouping options for stacks through "View > Group Stacks By." New files added to the desktop will be automatically sorted into the appropriate stack.

This setup helps you efficiently navigate and manage your MacBook Pro's desktop environment.

FINDER

The Finder, represented by the blue icon with a smiling face, is the central hub for managing and accessing everything on your Mac. Here's how you can use the Finder effectively:

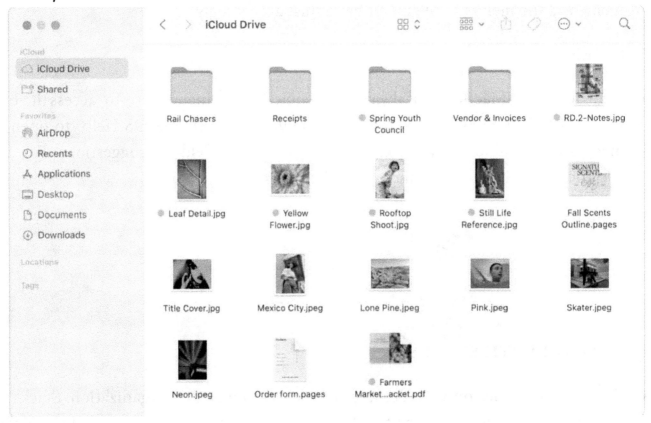

OPENING FINDER

- To open a Finder window, simply click the Finder icon in the Dock at the bottom of the screen.

NAVIGATING FINDER

- The Finder window provides various ways to view documents and folders. You can choose to view them as icons, in a list, in hierarchical columns, or in a gallery. You can change the view by clicking the pop-up menu button at the top of the Finder window.

SIDEBAR

The sidebar on the left side of the Finder window displays items you frequently use or want quick access to. For instance, the iCloud Drive folder shows all your documents stored in iCloud Drive. To customize the sidebar, go to Finder > Preferences.

ORGANIZING FOLDERS

- Your Mac comes with pre-created folders for different types of content, such as Documents, Pictures, Applications, and Music. You can also create new folders to keep your files organized. To create a new folder, go to File > New Folder.

SYNCING DEVICES

- When you connect devices like an iPhone or iPad, they appear in the Finder sidebar. Click the device's name to access options for backup, updates, synchronization, and restoration.

GALLERY VIEW

- Gallery View allows you to view a large preview of selected files, making it easier to visually identify images, video clips, and other documents. The Preview pane on the right provides additional information about the selected file. You can use the scrubber bar at the bottom to quickly navigate through your files.

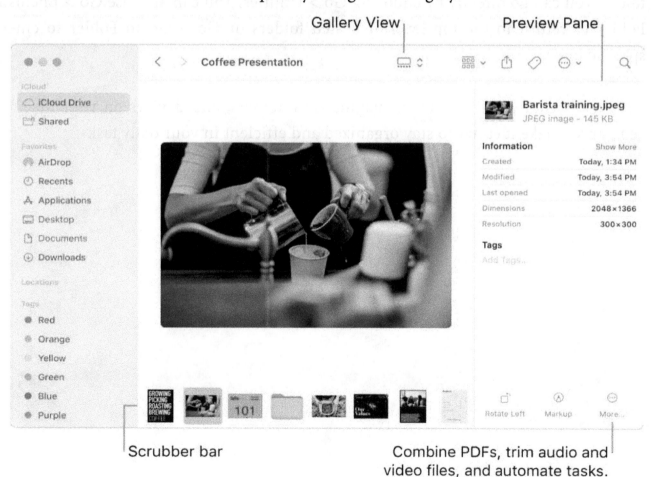

Gallery View   Preview Pane

Scrubber bar

Combine PDFs, trim audio and video files, and automate tasks.

QUICK ACTIONS

- In Gallery View, you can click the "More" button ⋯ at the bottom right of the Finder window to access shortcuts for managing and editing files directly in the Finder. These actions include rotating images, annotating or cropping images using Markup, combining images and PDFs into a single file, trimming audio and video files, running shortcuts created with the Shortcuts app, and creating custom actions with Automator workflows.

QUICK LOOK

- To quickly preview a file, select it and press the Space bar. Quick Look allows you to perform actions like signing PDFs, trimming audio and video files, marking up, rotating, and cropping images without opening a separate application.

GO MENU

- The Go menu in the menu bar provides a quick way to navigate to folders and locations. For example, instead of clicking through multiple folders to find the Utilities folder, you can go directly by choosing Go > Utilities. You can also use Go > Enclosing Folder to return to the top level of nested folders or Go > Go to Folder to enter a specific folder path.

The Finder is your go-to tool for managing files, folders, and devices on your Mac, and these features make it easier to stay organized and efficient in your daily tasks.

THE DOCK

The Dock on your Mac is a handy tool for accessing frequently used apps and features.

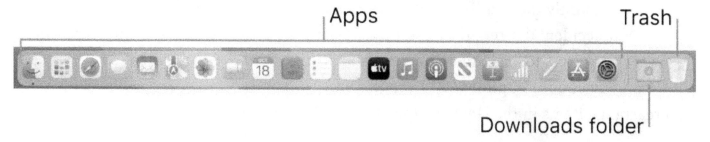

OPENING ITEMS IN THE DOCK

- To open an app, simply click on its icon in the Dock. For example, to open the Finder, click the ![icon] in the Dock.
- You can also open a file in an app by dragging the file over the app's icon in the Dock. For instance, to open a document in Pages, drag the document over the Pages icon in the Dock.
- To show an item in the Finder, Command-click the item's icon in the Dock.
- To switch to the previous app and hide the current app, Option-click the current app's icon.
- If you want to switch to another app and hide all other apps, Option-Command-click the icon of the app you want to switch to.

TAKING OTHER ACTIONS FOR ITEMS IN THE DOCK

- Control-click an item in the Dock to display a shortcut menu of actions. You can choose actions like "Show Recents" or click a filename to open the file.
- If an app becomes unresponsive, you can force it to quit by Control-clicking its icon in the Dock and selecting "Force Quit" (be aware that you may lose unsaved changes).

ADDING, REMOVING, OR REARRANGING DOCK ITEMS

- To add an item to the Dock, simply drag apps to the left side of the line that separates the recently used

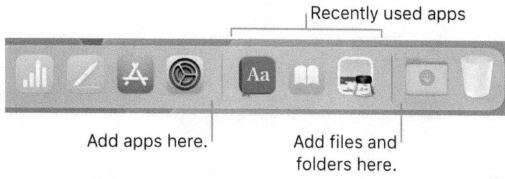

apps, or drag files and folders to the right side of the line. An alias for the item is placed in the Dock.

- To remove an item from the Dock, drag it out of the Dock until you see "Remove." Note that only the alias is removed; the actual item remains on your Mac.
- If you accidentally remove an app icon from the Dock, you can easily put it back. Open the app to make its icon reappear in the Dock, then Control-click the app's icon and choose "Options" > "Keep in Dock."

- To rearrange items in the Dock, simply drag an item to a new location.

CUSTOMIZING THE DOCK

- To customize the Dock's appearance and behavior, go to Apple menu > System Preferences, then click on "Desktop & Dock" in the sidebar. You may need to scroll down to find it.
- In the "Dock" preferences, you can change how items appear in the Dock, adjust its size, choose its location (bottom, left, or right edge of the screen), or even hide it.
- Click the "Help" button at the bottom of the window to learn more about the available options.
- You can also quickly adjust the Dock's size by moving the pointer over the separator line in the Dock until a double arrow appears, then click and drag the pointer up or down.
- To navigate the Dock using keyboard shortcuts, press Control-F3 (or Control-Fn-F3 on a Mac laptop) to move to the Dock, then use the Left Arrow and Right Arrow keys to navigate between icons. Press Return to open an item.

RED BADGES IN THE DOCK

- A red badge on an icon in the Dock indicates that you have one or more pending actions in an app or System Preferences. For instance, a red badge on the Mail icon indicates that you have new emails to read.

NOTIFICATION CENTRE

Notification Centre on your Mac is a handy tool for managing notifications and accessing widgets for various purposes.

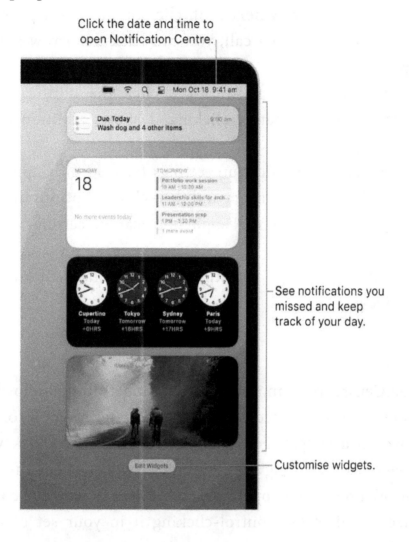

Click the date and time to open Notification Centre.

See notifications you missed and keep track of your day.

Customise widgets.

OPENING AND CLOSING NOTIFICATION CENTRE

- To open Notification Centre, click the date and time in the menu bar at the top-right corner of your screen. Alternatively, you can swipe left with two fingers from the right edge of the trackpad.
- To close Notification Centre, you can click anywhere on the desktop, click the date and time in the menu bar again, or swipe right with two fingers toward the right edge of the trackpad.

USING NOTIFICATIONS

- In Notification Centre, move your pointer over a notification to interact with it in various ways:

- To expand or collapse a stack of notifications from a single app, click anywhere in the top notification to expand it or click "Show less" to collapse the stack.
- You can take action directly from a notification by clicking on the action, such as Snooze in a Calendar notification or Reply in a Mail notification.
  - If an action has a ⌄ arrow next to it, clicking the arrow provides more options. For example, in response to a call, you can click the arrow next to Decline, then choose Reply with Message.
- To see more details about a notification, click the notification itself. If there's a ⟩ arrow next to the app name, clicking it shows additional details within the notification.
- If you want to adjust the notification settings for a specific app, click the ⟩ next to the app name, click the ••• button, and then choose options like muting or turning off notifications or accessing the app's notification settings in the Notifications preferences.
- To clear a single notification or all notifications in a stack, click the ⊗ or "Clear All" button, respectively.

USING WIDGETS:

- In Notification Centre, you can interact with widgets in the following ways:
  - To see more details or access related preferences, apps, or web pages, click anywhere within a widget. For example, clicking in a Clock widget opens Date & Time preferences, clicking the Reminders widget opens the Reminders app, or clicking the Weather widget opens a web browser to view the complete forecast.
- You can resize a widget by Control-clicking it in your set of active widgets and choosing a different size.
- If you want to remove a widget, press and hold the Option key while hovering over the widget, then click the "Remove" ⊖ button.

CONTROL CENTRE

Control Center on your Mac is a convenient way to access various settings and controls right from the menu bar.

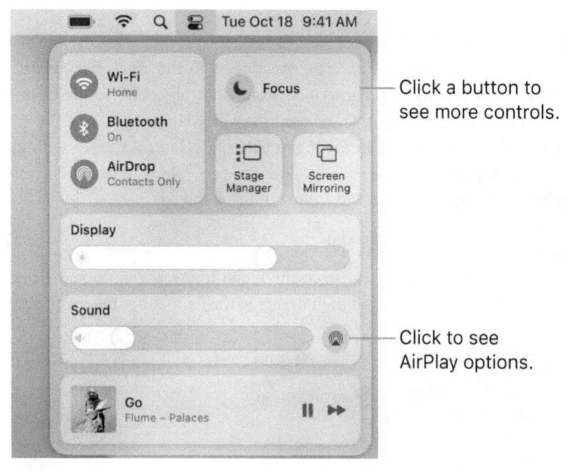

1. **Open Control Center**
   - Click the Control Center icon located in the upper-right corner of your Mac's screen. It looks like a series of icons.

2. **Access More Options**
   - Clicking a button in Control Center allows you to access a set of related options or settings. For example, if you click the Wi-Fi button 📶, you can view available Wi-Fi networks, your preferred networks, or open Wi-Fi Settings. To return to the main Control Center view, click the Control Center icon again.

3. **Manage Your Desktop with Stage Manager**
   - Use Stage Manager to organize your apps and windows in a single view and switch between them quickly. You can group apps together to create workspaces that suit your workflow. This feature is especially useful for managing multiple open apps and windows efficiently.

4. Monitor Your Microphone

- The recording indicator in Control Center shows when your Mac's microphone is in use or if it was recently used. This visual indicator enhances security and privacy by informing you when an app has access to the microphone.

5. Pin Your Control Center Favorites

- You can pin your favorite Control Center items to the menu bar for quick access. To do this, simply drag a favorite item from Control Center to the menu bar. This allows you to access frequently used controls with a single click.
- To customize what appears in the menu bar, open Control Center settings, and use the dropdown menu next to each module to select "Show in Menu Bar." You'll see a preview of where the control will appear in the menu bar.

6. Removing Items from the Menu Bar

- If you want to remove an item from the menu bar, you can do so by pressing and holding the Command key and then dragging the item out of the menu bar.

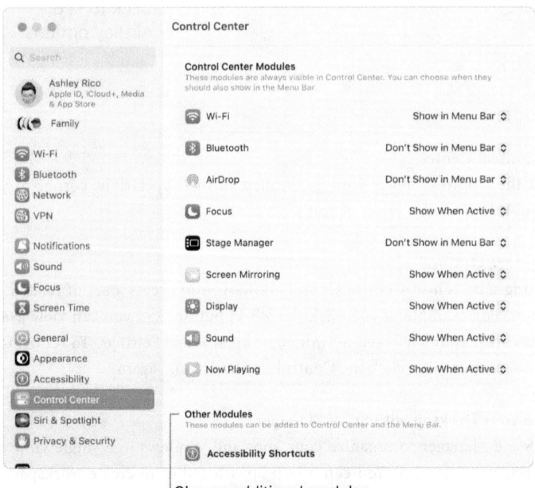

Choose additional modules
to add to Control Center.

SYSTEM SETTINGS

System Settings on your Mac allow you to personalize and configure various aspects of your MacBook. Here's how you can use System Settings:

1. **Accessing System Settings**
   - To access System Settings, you can do one of the following:
     - Click the System Settings ⚙ in the Dock.
     - Choose "Apple menu > System Preferences" from the top-left corner of your screen, and then select the setting you want to adjust from the sidebar.

1. **Customizing Your MacBook**
   - Within System Settings, you can customize various settings related to your MacBook. These settings cover a wide range of options, including but not limited to:
     - Lock Screen settings: Adjust when your Mac goes to sleep.
     - Wallpaper settings: Set a custom desktop background.
     - Appearance settings: Choose between light mode, dark mode, or auto mode for your Mac's appearance.

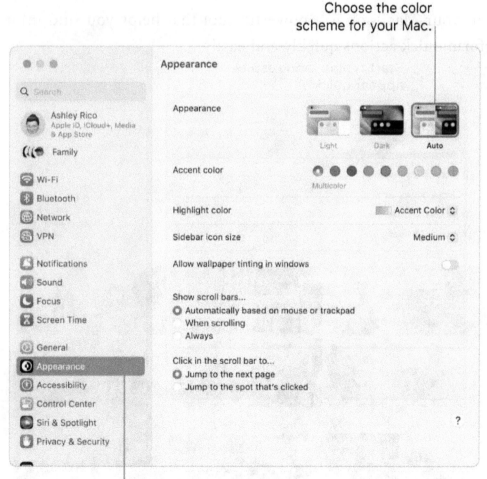

Choose the color scheme for your Mac.

Click an item in the sidebar to adjust settings.

- To make adjustments, click on the specific setting in the sidebar that you want to customize. Depending on your preference, you may need to scroll down to see additional settings.

3. **Updating macOS**
   - In System Settings, you can also check for and update your macOS software. Here's how:
     - Click on "General" in the System Settings window.
     - Then, click on "Software Update" to see if your Mac is running the latest version of macOS software.
     - You can specify preferences for automatic software updates as well.

Using System Settings, you can tailor your MacBook to suit your preferences and stay up to date with the latest macOS software updates. It's a crucial tool for managing the configuration and appearance of your Mac.

SPOTLIGHT ON YOUR MAC

Spotlight $\mathbb{Q}$ on your MacBook is a powerful tool that helps you find information, open apps, and perform quick actions quickly and easily.

1. Accessing Spotlight

- Click on the Spotlight icon at the top right of your screen. You can also press the Spotlight key (F4) on your keyboard if you have a 14-inch or 16-inch MacBook.
- To quickly show or hide the Spotlight search field, you can use the keyboard shortcut Command–Space bar.

2. Searching for Anything

- Once you open Spotlight, start typing what you're looking for. Spotlight will instantly display search results that match your query. You can search for various types of content, including images, documents, contacts, calendar events, and email messages.
- With Live Text, Spotlight can even search for text within images. Please note that not all languages may be supported for this feature.

3. Opening Apps

- To quickly open an app, simply type its name in Spotlight, and when you see it in the search results, press the Return key.

4. Performing Quick Actions

- Spotlight allows you to perform quick actions directly. For instance, you can run a shortcut, start a Focus mode, or set an alarm without opening additional apps.
- To use these quick actions, open Spotlight, then type the action you want to perform. For example, you can type "Clock" and choose "Create Timer" to set a timer right from Spotlight.

5. Currency and Measurement Conversions

- You can use Spotlight to convert currencies and measurements. Simply enter a currency symbol (e.g., $, €, or ¥) followed by an amount, and then press Return. Spotlight will display a list of converted values.
- For measurement conversions, specify a unit of measure, and Spotlight will provide the converted result.

6. Siri Suggestions

- Spotlight also offers Siri Suggestions, which provide information from various sources such as Wikipedia articles, web search results, news, sports, weather, stocks, movies, and more when you perform a search.

7. Customizing Spotlight

- If you want Spotlight to search only for items on your MacBook and not fetch suggestions from the web, you can customize its behavior. Go to "System Preferences > Siri & Spotlight" and deselect "Siri Suggestions" in the list of Search Results. You can make other changes to the categories that Spotlight searches as well.

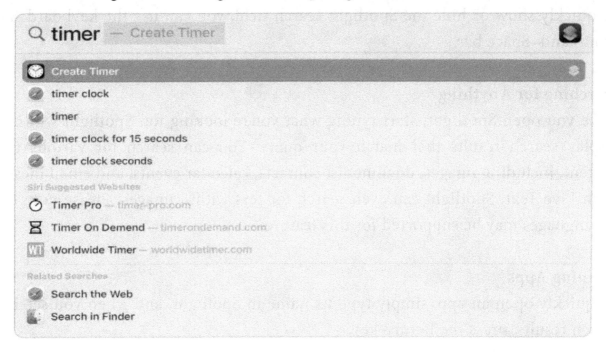

SIRI ON YOUR MAC

Siri is a powerful virtual assistant on your MacBook that you can use to perform various tasks using your voice. Here's how to enable and use Siri effectively:

ENABLE AND ACTIVATE SIRI

- Open "System Preferences" on your MacBook.
- Click on "Siri & Spotlight."
- Set your Siri preferences, including the language and voice you prefer.
- To activate Siri, you can:
  - On a 13-inch MacBook Pro: Tap the Siri button ⬤ in the Control Strip on the Touch Bar or press and hold the Command-Space bar.
  - On a 14-inch or 16-inch MacBook Pro: Press and hold the Dictation/Siri (F5) key or the microphone key 🎤 on the keyboard to open Siri.
  - You can also click "Siri & Spotlight" in System Preferences, then select "Ask Siri."

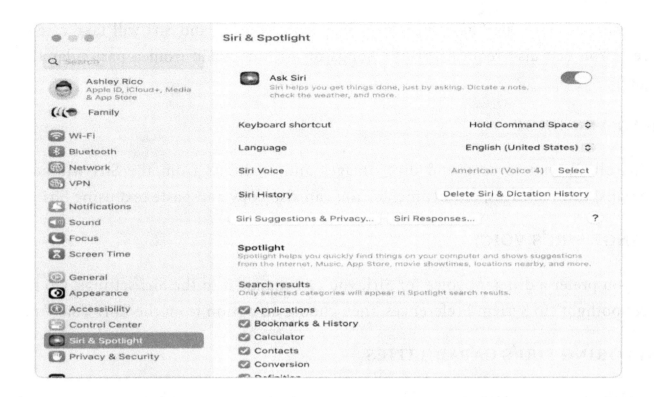

HEY SIRI!

- To use the "Hey Siri" feature, which allows you to activate Siri by voice, go to Siri settings and click "Listen for 'Hey Siri.'" Follow the prompts to set it up.
- Once enabled, you can simply say "Hey Siri" followed by your request to get a response.
- Note that "Hey Siri" won't respond when the MacBook 's lid is closed for convenience.

3. USING SIRI

You can use Siri for a wide range of tasks, including:

- Scheduling meetings and appointments.
- Changing system settings.
- Getting answers to questions.
- Sending messages.
- Making calls.
- Adding items to your calendar.
- Providing directions.
- Offering information on various topics.
- Performing basic tasks like creating lists.

PLAY MUSIC

- To play music using Siri, simply say "Play some music," and Siri will take care of the rest. You can also request specific songs or ask for music from a particular time or genre.

DRAG AND DROP

- Siri allows you to drag and drop images and locations from the Siri window into emails, text messages, or documents. You can also copy and paste text using Siri.

CHANGE SIRI'S VOICE

- If you prefer a different voice for Siri, you can change it in the Siri settings. Go to "Siri & Spotlight" in System Preferences, then choose an option from the "Siri Voice" menu.

EXPLORING SIRI'S CAPABILITIES

- To discover more ways to use Siri, you can simply ask Siri, "What can you do?" at any time. Siri will provide you with a list of tasks and functions it can perform.

WINDOW MANAGEMENT ON YOUR MAC

Window management is crucial for efficiently organizing and navigating open apps and windows on your Mac.

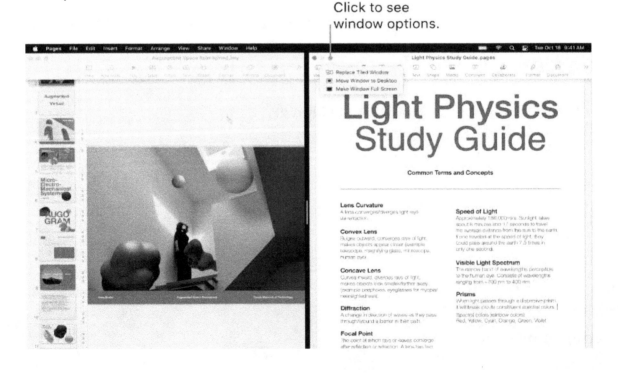

USE FULL SCREEN VIEW

- To make an app occupy the entire screen, enter full-screen view.
- Move the pointer over the green button in the top-left corner of the app window.
- Choose "Enter Full Screen" from the menu that appears.
- In full-screen view, the menu bar is hidden until you move the pointer to the top of the screen.
- This is particularly useful for apps like Keynote, Numbers, and Pages.

USE SPLIT VIEW

- Split View allows you to work with two app windows side by side, both filling the screen.
- Move the pointer over the green button in the top-left corner of a window you want to use.
- Choose "Tile Window to Left of Screen" or "Tile Window to Right of Screen" from the menu.
- Click another window to automatically fill the other half of the screen.
- The menu that appears when the pointer is over the green button offers options to switch apps and more.

STAGE MANAGER

- Stage Manager is a feature in Control Center that automatically organizes your apps and windows to keep your desktop clutter-free.
- The focused window is front and center, while other windows are arranged on the side for easy access.
- You can access Stage Manager from Control Center.

MISSION CONTROL

- Mission Control is a powerful tool for managing open windows. It displays all open windows in a single layer.
- You can access Mission Control by pressing the Mission Control key ⊟☐ on your keyboard or by pressing Control-Up Arrow.
- You can also add the Mission Control icon ⊞ to the Dock for quick access.
- It's useful for quickly finding and switching between open windows and desktop spaces.

MULTIPLE DESKTOP SPACES

- Organize your app windows into multiple desktop spaces to manage different tasks separately.
- To create a new space, enter Mission Control and click the "Add Desktop" ✛ button.
- You can switch between spaces using keyboard shortcuts and Mission Control.
- Dragging windows from one space to another is also possible.

USING THE TRAFFIC LIGHT BUTTONS

- The red, yellow, and green buttons in the top-left corner of every window have specific functions.
- Red: Closes the app window. In some apps, it quits the app entirely.
- Yellow: Minimizes the window to the right side of the Dock. Click it in the Dock to reopen it.
- Green: Maximizes the window to full screen or enters Split View, among other functions.

TRANSFER YOUR DATA TO YOUR NEW MACBOOK

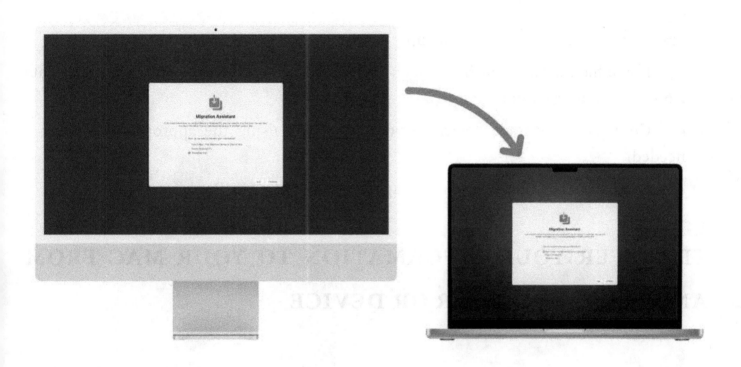

TO TRANSFER YOUR DATA TO YOUR NEW MACBOOK, FOLLOW THESE STEPS

1. Check macOS Versions

   • Ensure that your older computer is running macOS 10.7 or later. It's advisable to update your older computer to the latest macOS version if possible.

2. Prepare Your New MacBook

   • Make sure your new MacBook is running the latest version of macOS. To check for updates, go to System Preferences > General > Software Update.

3. Wireless Transfer

   - You can use Migration Assistant to transfer data wirelessly from another Mac or PC to your MacBook.

   - Open Finder, go to Applications, and open the Utilities folder.

   - Double-click on Migration Assistant and follow the onscreen instructions.

   - Ensure that both computers are connected to the same network and keep them near each other during the migration process.

4. Transfer from Time Machine Backup

   - If you have a Time Machine backup on a USB storage device, you can transfer data from it to your MacBook.

   - Connect the storage device to your MacBook using the appropriate adapter if needed.

   - Drag and drop files from the storage device to your MacBook.

TRANSFER YOUR INFORMATION TO YOUR MAC FROM ANOTHER COMPUTER OR DEVICE

To transfer your information to your Mac from another computer or device, follow these steps:

TRANSFER FROM A MAC

1. Upgrade both Mac computers to the latest version of macOS.
2. Connect the two computers using a cable (Ethernet, FireWire, or Thunderbolt) or ensure they're on the same network.
3. Open System Preferences on your new Mac, click on General, then select "Transfer or Reset" on the right and click "Open Migration Assistant."
4. Click Continue and follow the onscreen instructions.
5. On the other Mac, open Migration Assistant and follow the onscreen instructions.
6. Select the information you want to transfer:

   - Apps
   - User accounts (and specific content like apps, documents, etc.)

- Documents and files from apps
- Computer settings

7. Follow any additional instructions and click Continue to start the transfer.
8. Once completed, review the migration summary for any issues and click Done to exit Migration Assistant.

TRANSFER FROM A PC

1. Ensure both computers are on the same network (wired or wireless).
2. Download and install the Windows Migration Assistant for your macOS version on your PC.
3. Close any open Windows apps on your PC.
4. Open Windows Migration Assistant and follow the onscreen instructions.
5. Select the information to transfer:
   - User accounts (and specific content)
   - Computer settings
   - Additional shared files, apps, and documents
6. Click Continue to start the transfer.
7. Once completed, click Done to exit Migration Assistant.

TRANSFER FROM A TIME MACHINE BACKUP OR STORAGE DEVICE

1. Connect the storage device to your Mac (using an appropriate adapter if needed).
2. Open System Preferences on your new Mac, click on General, then select "Transfer or Reset" on the right and click "Open Migration Assistant."
3. Click Continue and follow the onscreen instructions.
4. Select the information you want to transfer.
5. Follow any additional instructions and click Continue to start the transfer.
6. Once completed, review the migration summary for any issues and click Done to exit Migration Assistant.

TRANSFER YOUR DATA TO A NEW MAC USING MIGRATION ASSISTANT

To transfer your data to a new Mac using Migration Assistant, follow these steps:

ON YOUR NEW MAC:

1. Open Migration Assistant on your new Mac. You can find it in the Utilities folder within the Applications folder.
2. When prompted for permission to make changes, enter your administrator password and click "OK."
3. Choose the option to transfer from a Mac, Time Machine backup, or startup disk and click "Continue."

ON YOUR OLD MAC

4. Open Migration Assistant on your old Mac, located in the Utilities folder within the Applications folder, and click "Continue."
5. Select the option to transfer to another Mac and click "Continue."

BACK ON YOUR NEW MAC:

6. When asked to select a source, choose the old Mac and click "Continue."

ON YOUR OLD MAC:

7. If you see a security code, ensure it matches the one displayed on your new Mac and click "Continue."

BACK ON YOUR NEW MAC

8. Migration Assistant will catalog the content on your old Mac and calculate the storage space used by apps, user accounts, files, folders, and settings. This process may take a few minutes.

9. Select the specific information you want to transfer, such as user accounts and folders.

10. Before clicking "Continue," consider what to do if there are accounts with the same name on both Macs:

  • Rename: The account on your old Mac will appear as an additional user on your new Mac with a separate login and home folder.

  • Replace: The account on your old Mac will replace the identically named account on your new Mac.

11. Initiate the transfer by clicking "Continue." Large transfers may take hours to complete, so you might want to start in the evening and allow it to finish overnight.

AFTER THE TRANSFER

12. Once Migration Assistant finishes, close it on both computers.

13. Log in to the migrated account on your new Mac to access its files and settings.

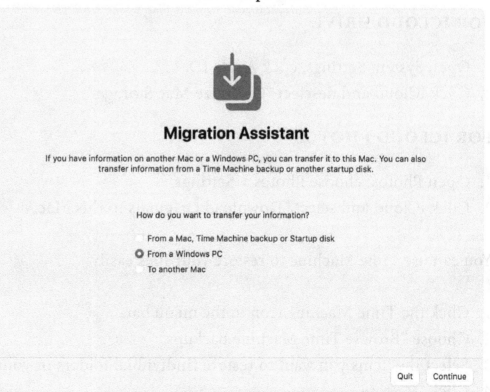

Migration Assistant

If you have information on another Mac or a Windows PC, you can transfer it to this Mac. You can also transfer information from a Time Machine backup or another startup disk.

How do you want to transfer your information?

From a Mac, Time Machine backup or Startup disk
◉ From a Windows PC
To another Mac

Quit   Continue

BACKING UP YOUR MACBOOK WITH TIME MACHINE

To keep your files safe, it's essential to back up your MacBook regularly. The easiest way to do this is by using Time Machine, which is built into your Mac. Time Machine can back up your apps, accounts, settings, music, photos, movies, and documents (excluding the macOS operating system). You can back up to an external storage device connected to your MacBook or a supported network volume. Check Apple Support for a list of devices compatible with Time Machine.

SETTING UP TIME MACHINE

Ensure your MacBook is on the same Wi-Fi network as your external storage device, or connect the external storage device to your MacBook.

1. Open System Settings, click General > Time Machine.
2. Click "Add Backup Disk."
3. Select the drive you want to use for backup, and you're all set.

Files in iCloud Drive and photos in iCloud Photos are automatically stored in iCloud and don't need to be part of your Time Machine backup. However, if you want to back them up:

FOR ICLOUD DRIVE

1. Open System Settings, click Apple ID.
2. Click iCloud and deselect "Optimize Mac Storage."

FOR ICLOUD PHOTOS

1. Open Photos, choose Photos > Settings.
2. Click iCloud and select "Download Originals to this Mac."

You can use Time Machine to restore your files easily:

1. Click the Time Machine icon in the menu bar.
2. Choose "Browse Time Machine backups."
3. Select the items you want to restore (individual folders or your entire disk).
4. Click "Restore."

Note: If your operating system or startup disk is damaged, you must first reinstall macOS before restoring your files using Time Machine.

TO RESTORE YOUR MAC TO ITS ORIGINAL STATE(WARNING: ERASING YOUR MAC REMOVES ALL THE INFORMATION FROM IT. BEFORE YOU START, BACK UP YOUR MAC WITH TIME MACHINE.)

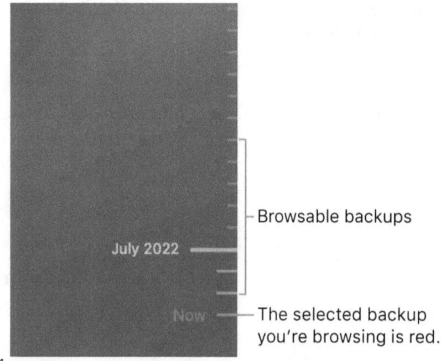

Browsable backups

The selected backup you're browsing is red.

On a Mac with Apple silicon or an Intel-based Mac with the Apple T2 Security Chip, use Erase Assistant to reset your Mac to factory settings before you trade it in or sell it. You can also use Erase Assistant to erase your Mac before reinstalling macOS. Erase Assistant removes your content and settings, and any apps that you installed.

What does Erase Assistant do?

Erase Assistant does the following things on your Mac:

- Signs you out of Apple services, such as iCloud.
- Turns off Find My and Activation Lock, so the Mac you're erasing is no longer associated with you.
- Erases your content and settings, and any apps that you installed.
- Erases all volumes (not just the volume you're on). If you installed Windows on your Mac using Boot Camp Assistant, the BOOTCAMP volume is also erased.
- Erases all user accounts and their data (not just your own user account).

ERASE YOUR MAC

1. Choose Apple menu > System Preferences.
2. In the menu bar, choose System Preferences > Erase All Content and Settings.

3. In Erase Assistant, enter your administrator information.
4. Review items that will be removed in addition to your content and settings.
5. If your Mac has multiple user accounts, click the arrow next to your account name to review the items.
6. Click Continue, then follow the on-screen instructions.

Note: If your version of macOS has been modified, Erase Assistant can't erase your Mac and displays an alert indicating you need to first reinstall macOS. Reinstall macOS, then use Erase Assistant.

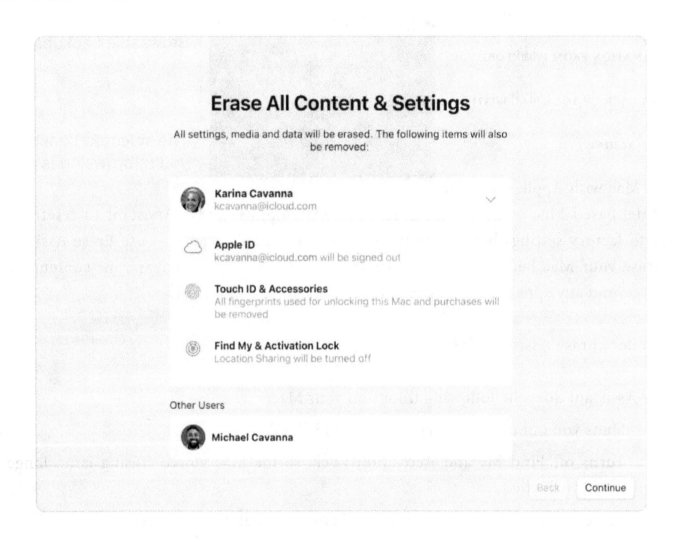

CONNECTING YOUR MAC WITH OTHER DEVICES

AIRDROP ON YOUR MAC

USING AIRDROP TO SHARE CONTENT

1. Open the file you want to send, then click the Share button. For files in the Finder, you can also Control-click the file, then choose "Share" from the shortcut menu.
2. Choose "AirDrop" from the sharing options listed.
3. A recipient list will appear in the AirDrop sheet. You can select a recipient from this list.

Alternatively, you can open an AirDrop window by selecting "AirDrop" in the sidebar of a Finder window or choosing "Go > AirDrop" from the menu bar.

The AirDrop window will display nearby AirDrop users. To send files, drag one or more documents, photos, or other files to the recipient's name shown in the window.

RECEIVING CONTENT WITH AIRDROP

1. When someone nearby attempts to send you a file using AirDrop, you'll see their request as a notification or as a message in the AirDrop window.
2. Click "Accept" to save the file to your Downloads folder.

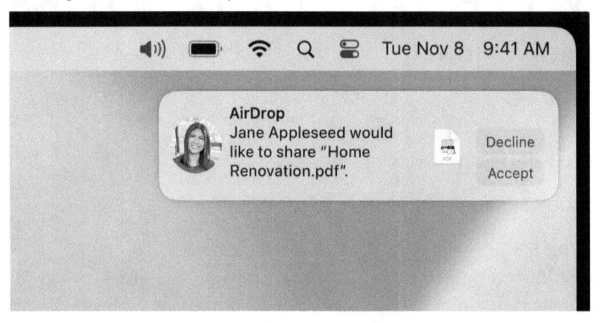

TROUBLESHOOTING IF YOU CAN'T SEE THE OTHER DEVICE IN AIRDROP

1. Ensure that both devices are within 9 meters (30 feet) of each other and have Wi-Fi and Bluetooth turned on.
2. Choose "Go > AirDrop" from the menu bar in the Finder on your Mac, then tick the "Allow me to be discovered by" setting in the AirDrop window. iPhone, iPad, and iPod touch have a similar setting. If set to receive from "Contacts Only," both devices must be signed in to iCloud, and the sender's Apple ID email address or phone number must be in the Contacts app of the receiving device.
3. Install the latest software updates for your Mac and other devices.
4. Make sure that incoming connections aren't blocked in firewall settings:

   • For macOS Ventura or later: Choose Apple menu > System Settings, click "Network" in the sidebar, then click "Firewall" on the right. Click the "Options" button, and ensure that "Block all incoming connections" is turned off.

   • For earlier versions of macOS: Choose Apple menu > System Preferences, then click "Security & Privacy." Click the "Firewall" tab, click the lock icon and enter your administrator password when prompted. Click "Firewall Options," then make sure that "Block all incoming connections" is deselected.

AIRPLAY TO MAC

You can also airplay videos or movies from your iPad or iPhone to your Mac. See below:

STREAM VIDEO FROM IPHONE OR IPAD

1. Ensure your device is connected to the same Wi-Fi network as your Apple TV, AirPlay-compatible smart TV, or Mac.

2. Find the video you want to stream on your iPhone or iPad.

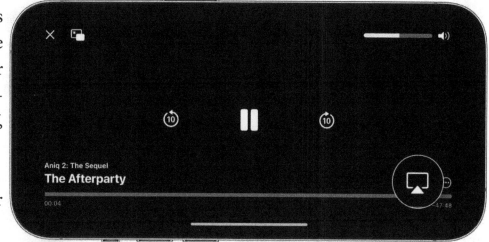

3. Tap the AirPlay button. In some apps, you may need to tap a different button first. For example, in the Photos app, tap the Share button, then tap the AirPlay button.

4. Choose your TV or Mac from the list of available devices.

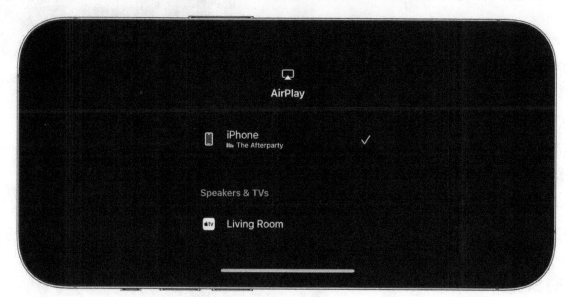

5. To stop streaming, tap the AirPlay button in the app you're using, then select your iPhone or iPad from the list.

STREAM VIDEO AUTOMATICALLY

Depending on your settings, your iPhone or iPad can suggest or automatically connect to devices you use with AirPlay regularly. Here's how to adjust these settings:

1. Go to Settings 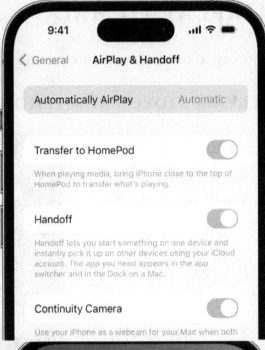 on your iPhone or iPad.
2. Tap General.
3. Tap AirPlay & Handoff, then tap "Automatically AirPlay."
4. Choose a setting:

   • Never: Manually choose a device for AirPlay.

   • Ask: Get suggested AirPlay connection notifications.

   • Automatic: Get suggested and automatic AirPlay connection notifications.

   •

Ensure both your iPhone or iPad and your AirPlay-enabled device are on the same Wi-Fi network for automatic and suggested AirPlay connections.

MIRROR IPHONE OR IPAD TO A TV OR MAC

1. Connect your iPhone or iPad to the same Wi-Fi network as your Apple TV, AirPlay-compatible smart TV, or Mac.
2. Open Control Centre:

   • On iPhone X or later, or iPad with iPadOS 13 or later: Swipe down from the upper right-hand corner of the screen.

   • On iPhone 8 or earlier or iOS 11 or earlier: Swipe up from the bottom edge of the screen.
3. Tap the Screen Mirroring button 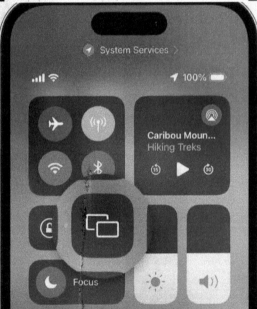.
4. Select your TV or Mac from the list of available devices.
5. If an AirPlay passcode appears on your TV screen or Mac, enter the passcode on your iPhone or iPad.
6. To stop mirroring, open Control Centre, tap Screen Mirroring, then tap Stop Mirroring.

Alternatively, press the Menu button on your Apple TV Remote.

Please note that not all video apps support AirPlay, so be sure to check the App Store on your Apple TV for app availability. You can also find out which macOS versions and Mac models are compatible with AirPlay to Mac and how to set up your Mac as an AirPlay receiver if needed.

APPLEPAY ON YOUR MAC AND OTHER DEVICES

Shopping online using Apple Pay on your Mac and completing the purchase with your iPhone or Apple Watch is a convenient and secure way to make online transactions. Here's how you can do it:

STEP 1: SET UP APPLE PAY ON YOUR MAC

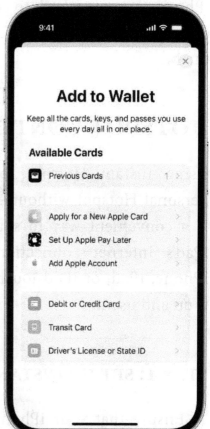

- Ensure you have Apple Pay set up on your Mac. You can do this by going to System ⚙ > "Wallet & Apple Pay."
- Add your debit or credit cards to Apple Pay by pressing on the add button ➕ on the top right of Wallet & Apple Pay on your Mac or other Apple device.

STEP 2: START SHOPPING ON YOUR MAC

1. Open your web browser on your Mac and go to the online store where you want to make a purchase.
2. Browse the website, select the items you wish to buy, and add them to your cart.
3. Proceed to the checkout page.

STEP 3: CHOOSE APPLE PAY

1. On the checkout page, look for the Apple Pay option.
2. Click on the Apple Pay button. This will initiate the payment process.

STEP 4: CONFIRM YOUR PURCHASE ON YOUR IPHONE OR APPLE WATCH

1. Shortly after clicking the Apple Pay button on your Mac, a payment prompt will appear

on your iPhone or Apple Watch if they are nearby and signed in to the same account. On your iPhone, use Face ID, Touch ID, or your passcode to authorize the payment.

2. On your Apple Watch, double-click the side button to confirm the payment.

STEP 5: COMPLETE THE TRANSACTION

1. Once you've confirmed the payment on your iPhone or Apple Watch, your Mac will receive the confirmation, and your purchase will be finalized.
2. You'll typically receive an email or on-screen confirmation of your successful transaction.

That's it! You've successfully shopped online on your Mac and used Apple Pay on your iPhone or Apple Watch to complete the purchase. This method ensures a quick and secure online shopping experience without the need to manually enter your payment details on the Mac.

HOTSPOT CONTINUITY

Using Instant Hotspot to connect to your Personal Hotspot without entering a password is a convenient way to share your iPhone or iPad's internet connection with your Mac, iPhone, iPad, or iPod touch. Here's how to set it up and use it:

STEP 1: SET UP INSTANT HOTSPOT

1. Ensure that your iPhone or iPad (Wi-Fi + Cellular) has an activated service provider plan that includes Personal Hotspot service.
2. Make sure all devices you want to connect are signed in to iCloud with the same Apple ID.
3. Enable Bluetooth and Wi-Fi on all devices involved.

STEP 2: USE INSTANT HOTSPOT

To connect from your Mac
1. Click on the Wi-Fi icon 🛜 in the Control Center or the menu bar ⬒ on your Mac.

2. You'll see the name of the iPhone or iPad providing your Personal Hotspot ⌇ listed there with a personal hotspot icon next to it.

3. Click on the name of your iPhone or iPad.

TO CONNECT FROM ANOTHER IPHONE OR IPAD

1. Open the "Settings" ⚙ app on your iPhone or iPad, tap "Wi-Fi."
2. You'll see the name of the iPhone or iPad providing your Personal Hotspot listed there with a personal hotspot icon next to it. Tap on the name of your iPhone or iPad.

CAMERA CONTINUITY

You can easily use your iPhone or iPad to scan documents or take pictures on your Mac using Continuity Camera. Here's how to do it:

STEP 1: USE AN APP THAT SUPPORTS CONTINUITY CAMERA

You can use Continuity Camera to scan or take a picture in these built-in apps on your Mac:

Finder	Notes
Keynote 8.2 or later	Numbers 5.2 or later
Mail	Pages 7.2 or later
Messages	TextEdit

STEP 2: TAKE A PHOTO

To take a photo and have it instantly appear on your Mac:

1. Open a supported app on your Mac.
2. You can either:

   • Control-click where you want the photo to be inserted in the app window. From the shortcut menu, choose "Insert from iPhone or iPad" > "Take Photo." You can do this in a Finder window or on the desktop.

   • From the File menu (or Insert menu, if applicable), choose "Insert from iPhone or iPad" > "Take Photo."

3. The Camera app will open on your iPhone or iPad.

4. Tap the Shutter button ⬤ to take a photo.

5. After taking the photo, tap "Use Photo" on your iPhone or iPad.

6. Your photo will instantly appear in the window on your Mac.

STEP 3: SCAN DOCUMENTS

To scan documents and have them appear on your Mac:

1. Open a supported app on your Mac.

2. You can either:

   • Control-click where you want the scan to be inserted in the app window. From the shortcut menu, choose "Insert from iPhone or iPad" > "Scan Documents." You can do this in a Finder window or on the desktop.

   • From the File menu (or Insert menu, if applicable), choose "Insert from iPhone or iPad" > "Scan Documents."

3. The Camera app will open on your iPhone or iPad.

4. Place your document in view of the camera and wait for the scan to complete.

5. If needed, tap the Shutter button ⬤ to manually capture a scan.

6. Adjust the scan to fit the page by dragging the corners, then tap "Keep Scan" to save it.

7. You can add additional scans to the document or tap "Save" when you're finished.

8. Your scans will appear as a PDF in the window on your Mac.

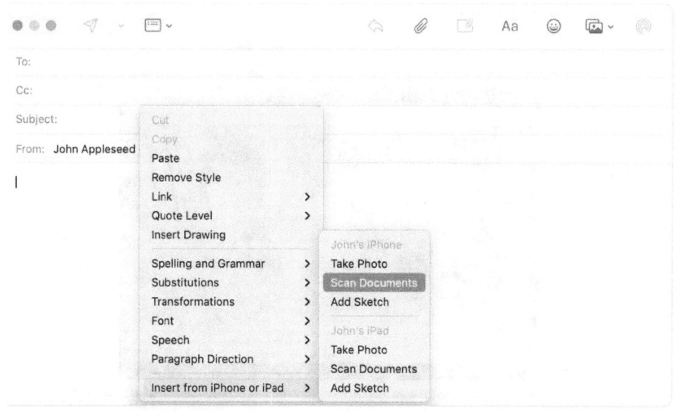

STEP 4: USE YOUR IPHONE AS A WEBCAM

You can also use your iPhone as a webcam for your Mac, but please note that this feature has different system requirements.

STEP 1: MOUNT YOUR IPHONE

Continuity Camera mounts and other iPhone-compatible mounts and stands are available from various manufacturers. When mounting your iPhone, make sure it meets the following criteria:

- It should be placed near your Mac.

- Ensure it's locked for security.

- Keep it stable to avoid movement.

- Position your iPhone with its rear cameras facing you and unobstructed.

- It can be mounted in landscape orientation to allow apps to choose your iPhone automatically, or in portrait orientation.

You can use Continuity Camera wired or wirelessly. To keep your iPhone charged while using it, you can plug it into your Mac or a USB charger. Your Mac will notify you if the iPhone battery level gets low.

STEP 2: CHOOSE YOUR IPHONE AS YOUR CAMERA OR MICROPHONE

When your iPhone is properly mounted, its camera and microphone are available to apps that can use them.

- To choose your iPhone camera, open an app like FaceTime or any other app that uses the camera. If the app doesn't automatically start using your iPhone camera, you can select it from the app's video menu or camera menu.
- To choose your iPhone microphone, go to Apple menu > System Settings, click on Sound in the sidebar, then select your iPhone microphone in the Input tab.

You don't need to manually select your iPhone microphone unless your Mac has no built-in or external microphone. In that case, your app might choose your iPhone microphone automatically.

Privacy Note: When the camera or microphone is in use, a privacy indicator appears in the iPhone status bar and next to Control Centre in the Mac menu bar. When used wirelessly, the iPhone emits a brief sound when an app begins using its camera or microphone.

STEP 3: USE EFFECTS AND FEATURES

macOS offers various video and audio features that you can use in FaceTime and many other video-conferencing apps. These features include Reactions, Presenter Overlay, camera modes, and microphone modes.

STEP 4: PAUSE, DISCONNECT, OR TURN OFF

If you receive a call while using your iPhone camera or microphone:

- If you answer the call on your iPhone, video and audio will pause until you end the call and lock and mount your iPhone.

- If you answer the call on your Mac, the current video and audio session pauses. When you end the call, you might need to choose your iPhone again in your app.

OTHER WAYS TO PAUSE, DISCONNECT, OR TURN OFF:

- Use your app's controls to stop video, mute audio, or end the call, or simply quit the app.

- Unlock your iPhone. To resume, lock and mount your iPhone. You may need to stop and restart video or audio in your app as well.

- Tap the Pause button on your iPhone screen. To resu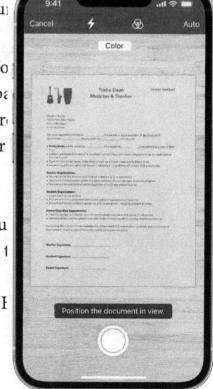 your iPhone.

- Tap the Disconnect button on your iPhone screen, o range of your Mac. The current video and audio session pა camera or microphone, if available. Your iPhone is r microphone lists on your Mac. To add it back, plug your mount your iPhone.

If you want to prevent your Mac from recognizing you microphone, even when it's plugged in and mounted, you can t

1. On your iPhone, go to Settings 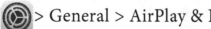 > General > AirPlay & F
2. Turn off Continuity Camera.

CONTINUITY CAMERA SYSTEM REQUIREMENTS

When used for scanning and taking photos on your Mac, Continuity Camera works with the following devices and operating systems:

- macOS Mojave or later	MacBook introduced in 2015 or later
MacBook Pro introduced in 2012 or later	MacBook Air introduced in 2012 or later
Mac mini introduced in 2012 or later	iMac introduced in 2012 or later
iMac Pro	Mac Pro introduced in 2013 or later
Mac Studio introduced in 2022 or later	iOS 12 or later
iPhone	iPad
iPod touch	

<table>
<tr><td colspan="2" align="center">Additional Requirements</td></tr>
<tr><td colspan="2">- Both devices must have both Wi-Fi and Bluetooth turned on.</td></tr>
<tr><td colspan="2">- Both devices must be signed in with the same Apple ID using two-factor authentication.</td></tr>
<tr><td colspan="2">- Ensure your Mac is using the latest version of macOS.</td></tr>
</table>

APPLE ID & ICLOUD SETTINGS

iCloud is a powerful service that keeps your important data safe, up-to-date, and accessible across all your Apple devices. It provides 5 GB of free storage for your files, documents and photos, and your purchases from Apple's digital stores don't count towards your available space. You can upgrade to iCloud+ for more storage and premium features.

SIGNING IN TO ICLOUD.COM

1. Open a web browser on your computer.
2. Go to [iCloud.com](https://www.icloud.com).
3. Sign in with your Apple ID using one of the following methods:

    • Enter your Apple ID (or a Reachable At email address or phone number associated with your Apple ID) and password.

    • If you're using Safari and are already signed in to a device that supports Face ID or Touch ID, you can use Face ID or Touch ID to sign in.

- In supported versions of Google Chrome or Microsoft Edge, you can enter your Apple ID and click "Sign in with Passkey" to scan a QR code (if you have iCloud Keychain enabled and an iPhone or iPad with iOS 17, iPadOS 17, or later).

4. If prompted, follow the on-screen instructions to verify your identity. This may involve entering a code sent to a trusted device or phone number, or using a security key. If you've lost your trusted device, you can use the "Find Devices" button for assistance.

APPS AND FEATURES AVAILABLE ON ICLOUD.COM

Once you sign in, you can access various apps and features on iCloud.com, depending on your account and device, such as:

SWITCHING BETWEEN APPS AND FEATURES ON ICLOUD.COM:

Once logged in to iCloud.com, using different apps and features is easy:

- Click on the app or feature tile on the iCloud.com homepage.

- You can also click within a tile, for instance, to open a specific note directly.

- Use the App Launcher button in the toolbar to select another app or feature.

SIGNING OUT OF ICLOUD.COM

To sign out of iCloud.com, follow these steps:

1. Click your Apple ID photo or the Account button in the top-right corner of the iCloud. com window.

2. Choose one of the following options:

- Sign out from the browser you're currently using: Select "Sign Out."

- Sign out from all browsers where you're signed in: Click "iCloud Settings," then "Sign Out Of All Browsers," and finally, "Sign Out."

Calendar	Contacts	Custom Email Domain (iCloud+)	Find Devices
Keynote	iCloud Mail	Hide My Email (iCloud+)	iCloud Drive
Notes	Numbers	Pages	Photos

SETTING UP ICLOUD DRIVE ON YOUR MAC OR WINDOWS COMPUTER

ON A MAC

macOS 13.3 or later:

1. Click the Apple menu  located at the top-left corner of your screen.
2. Choose "System Preferences."
3. Click on your name located at the top of the sidebar.
4. Click on "iCloud" on the right.
5. Select "iCloud Drive."
6. Turn on the "Sync this Mac" option.

macOS 13 to 13.2:

1. Click the Apple menu located at the top-left corner of your screen.
2. Choose "System Preferences."
3. Click on your name located at the top of the sidebar.
4. Click on "iCloud" on the right.
5. Select "iCloud Drive."
6. Click "Turn On."
7. Click "Options" to configure your preferences.

macOS 12 or earlier

1. Click the Apple menu located at the top-left corner of your screen.
2. Choose "System Preferences."
3. Click "Apple ID."
4. Click "iCloud."
5. Select "iCloud Drive."
6. Click "Options" to configure your preferences.

In the options, you have the ability to select or turn on various features, including "Desktop & Documents Folders," which allows you to access files on your desktop and in the Documents folder on any device with iCloud Drive enabled.

To access your iCloud Drive files and folders, open the Finder, and you'll find "iCloud Drive" in the sidebar.

ON A WINDOWS COMPUTER

If you're using a Windows computer, you can set up iCloud Drive by following these steps:

1. Download iCloud for Windows from the [official Apple website](https://support.apple.com/en-us/HT204283) if you haven't already.
2. Install and open iCloud for Windows.
3. Select "iCloud Drive," and then click "Apply."

To access your iCloud Drive files and folders on your Windows computer, open File Explorer, and you'll find "iCloud Drive" in the Navigation pane.

ACCESS DESKTOP AND DOCUMENTS FILES THROUGH ICLOUD DRIVE

ON YOUR MAC

1. Click on the Apple menu in the top-left corner of your screen.
2. Click on "System Preferences" Click on "Apple ID," then select "iCloud."
3. Ensure that iCloud Drive is turned on.
4. Click on "Options" next to iCloud Drive.
5. Choose "Desktop & Documents Folders."
6. Click "Done."

By doing this, your Desktop and Documents files will be synchronized with iCloud Drive, making them accessible from all your devices.

ON YOUR IPHONE, IPAD, AND IPOD TOUCH

To set up iCloud Drive on your iPhone, iPad, or iPod touch, follow these steps:

1. Open the Settings app  on your device.
2. Scroll down and tap on "[your name]" at the top of the settings.
3. Tap "iCloud."
4. Under "iCloud Drive," tap "Sync this [device]" to turn it on.

After you've turned on iCloud Drive, you can access your iCloud Drive files and folders by opening the "Files" app on your device. You'll find the iCloud Drive section within the app, where you can view and manage your files.

ON ICLOUD.COM

1. Sign in to iCloud.com using your Apple ID.
2. Go to iCloud Drive.
3. Double-click on the Desktop or Documents folder.
4. To use a file or make edits, click to download it. Once you've finished making edits, upload the file to iCloud Drive to ensure the latest version is available on all your devices.

By storing your files in iCloud Drive, you can save space on your devices. The files you keep in iCloud Drive use your iCloud storage, so ensure you have enough space available.

You can delete files in iCloud Drive to free up space, but keep in mind that when you delete a file on one device, it will be deleted on all devices signed in with the same Apple ID. Deleted files are stored in the "Recently Deleted" folder for 30 days before permanent removal.

TURNING OFF DESKTOP AND DOCUMENTS FEATURES:

1. Click on the Apple menu and select "System Preferences"
2. Click on "Apple ID," then select "iCloud."
3. Click on "Options" next to iCloud Drive.
4. Deselect "Desktop & Documents Folders."
5. Click "Done."

This will turn off the feature. Your files will remain in iCloud Drive, and a new Desktop and Documents folder will be created on your Mac in the home folder.

If you decide to turn off iCloud Drive or sign out of iCloud, a new Desktop and Documents folder will be created in your home folder, and you'll have the option to keep a local copy of your iCloud Drive files. These files will be copied to a folder called "iCloud Drive (Archive)" in your home folder. You can move any files that were in your iCloud Desktop and Documents to your new local Desktop and Documents.

HANDOFF ON MAC

If you have multiple Apple devices and want to seamlessly switch between them while using an app, you can use Handoff.

TO USE HANDOFF

1. Make sure that your devices meet the Continuity system requirements and have Wi-Fi, Bluetooth, and Handoff turned on.
2. Sign in with the same Apple ID on all your devices.

TO TURN HANDOFF ON OR OFF

On your Mac
1. Click on the Apple menu in the top-left corner of your screen.
2. Select System Preferences
3. Click on "General" in the sidebar.
4. In the "Allow Handoff between this Mac and your iCloud devices" section, turn the toggle on or off.

On your iOS or iPadOS device:

1. Open the Settings app 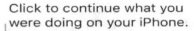 .
2. Scroll down and select "General."
3. Tap "AirPlay & Handoff."
4. Turn Handoff on or off.

Click to continue what you were doing on your iPhone.

On your Apple Watch (configured through your iPhone):

1. Open the Apple Watch app  on your iPhone.
2. Go to "My Watch."
3. Choose "General."
4. Turn "Enable Handoff" on or off.

TO HAND OFF AN APP FROM ONE DEVICE TO ANOTHER

From your Mac to an iOS or iPadOS device

The Handoff icon of the app you're using on your Mac will appear on your iPhone or iPad. You can continue working in the app by tapping on the Handoff icon.

From an iOS or iPadOS device or Apple Watch to your Mac

The Handoff icon of the app you're using on your iPhone, iPad, iPod touch, or Apple Watch will appear on your Mac's Dock. You can continue working in the app by clicking the Handoff icon.

You can also use the Command-Tab shortcut on your Mac's keyboard to quickly switch to the app that has the Handoff icon.

UNIVERSAL CLIPOARD

Universal Clipboard is a feature that allows you to seamlessly copy and paste content between your Apple devices, provided they are signed in with the same Apple ID and have the necessary settings turned on.

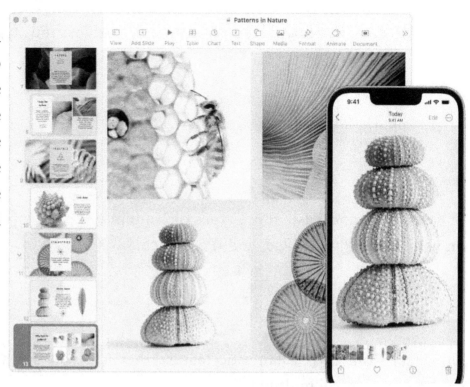

TO USE UNIVERSAL

CLIPBOARD

1. Ensure that your devices meet Continuity system requirements(Explored in Coninuity chapter).
2. Turn on Wi-Fi, Bluetooth, and Handoff in System Settings (on your Mac) and in Settings (on your iOS and iPadOS devices).
3. Sign in with the same Apple ID on all your devices.

COPYING ON A DEVICE

To copy content on a device, follow these steps:
1. Select the content you want to copy, just as you would with any copy action (e.g., on your Mac, press Command-C or choose Edit > Copy).
2. The copied content will be available for pasting on your other devices for a short time.

PASTING ON A DEVICE

1. Position the pointer or cursor where you want to paste the content.
2. Initiate the paste action. For example, on your iPad, you can double-tap and then choose "Paste" from the available options.

TYPES OF CONTENT

With Universal Clipboard, you can copy and paste various types of content, including:

- Text
- Images
- Photos
- Videos
- Files

You can copy and paste these types of content between apps that support copy and paste on your Mac, iPhone, iPad, and iPod touch.

UNIVERSAL CONTROL

Universal Control is a fantastic feature that lets you use a single keyboard, mouse, or trackpad to control multiple devices.

TO USE UNIVERSAL CONTROL

1. Check that your Mac has macOS version 12.3 or later, and your iPad has iPadOS 15.4 or later.
2. Ensure that both your devices have Bluetooth turned on and are connected to Wi-Fi.
3. Verify that Handoff is turned on in your General settings on your MacBook and in Settings > General > AirPlay & Handoff on your iPad.
4. Sign in with the same Apple ID on both devices and enable two-factor authentication.

CONNECTING DEVICES

1. Click on Control Center in the menu bar of your Mac.
2. Select "Screen Mirroring."
3. Under "Link Keyboard and Mouse," choose a device to link your keyboard and mouse to.

MOVING BETWEEN SCREENS

1. On your Mac, use your mouse or trackpad to move the pointer to the right or left edge of the screen closest to your iPad.
2. Pause briefly and then continue moving the pointer slightly past the edge of the screen.
3. When you see a border appear at the edge of the iPad screen, keep moving the pointer to the iPad screen.

DRAG AND DROP

1. Select the text, image, or object you want to move.
2. Drag it to the location on your other device where you want it to appear. For example, you can drag a sketch drawn with Apple Pencil from your iPad to the Keynote app on your MacBook. You can also copy content on one device and paste it on the other.

SHARING A KEYBOARD

1. With the pointer in a document or any area where you can enter text, start typing.
2. The keyboard input will be registered on the device where the pointer is active.

Universal Control is a simple yet powerful tool that lets you work seamlessly between your Mac and iPad. By following this guide, you can easily set it up and enjoy enhanced productivity and workflow.

HOW TO SET UP YOUR IPHONE TO MAKE PHONE CALLS AND SEND TEXT MESSAGES ON YOUR MAC

Using FaceTime on your Mac is a convenient way to have video or audio calls with friends and family.

MAKING A FACETIME CALL

1. Open the FaceTime app on your Mac.
2. Click the "New FaceTime" button to initiate a call.
3. Enter the name, email address, or phone number of the person you want to call.
4. Click the FaceTime button 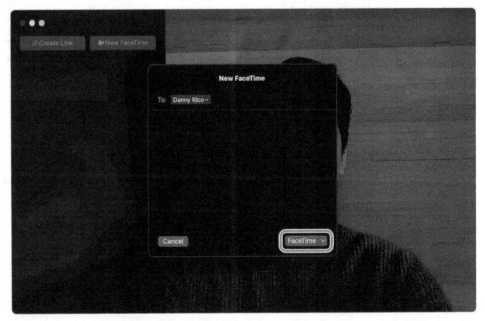 to make a video call. Alternatively, click the arrow ∨ next to it and choose FaceTime Audio for an audio call. If you can't see these options, click either the Video or Audio button.

If you're making a group call, you'll see a tile for each person in the group, which will say "Waiting" until they answer.

LEAVING A CALL

To leave a call, simply click the "End" button. If you leave a group call, others will remain on the call until they choose to leave.

MANAGING GROUP FACETIME CALLS:

During a Group FaceTime call, the video tiles work as follows:

- The most active speakers appear in live video tiles, while other participants are in a row of tiles below.

- You can click a tile to show that person's name, or double-click it to make the tile larger.

- A ⚠ symbol indicates a slow internet connection.

ADDING A PERSON TO A FACETIME CALL

1. While on a call, click the sidebar button ▤ in the FaceTime app and then click the add button . ⊕
2. Enter the new person's name, email, or phone number, and then click "Add."
3. Click the "Ring" button next to their name to call them. If a FaceTime link was created for the call, participants can share it to invite others to join.

USING FACETIME LINKS

FaceTime links simplify planning for calls and allow participants with Android and Windows devices to join via their web browser. Here's how to create and use FaceTime links:

1. Open the FaceTime app.
2. Click 🔗 to generate a sharing menu or choose other sharing options.
3. The link will appear in the FaceTime window's sidebar.
4. Double-click the FaceTime Link to start the call.
5. Participants who click the link need to be allowed into the call.

- To let a participant join the call, click the tick ✓ next to their name.

- If you want to decline a participant's request to join the call, click the decline button ✕ next to their name.

- If you need to remove a participant from the call within 30 seconds of them joining, click the remove button ⊗.

ANSWERING A FACETIME CALL

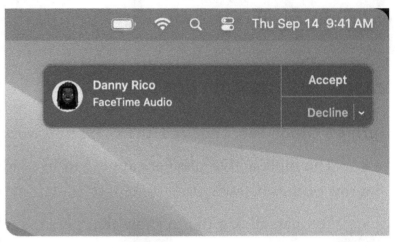

When you receive a FaceTime call, a notification will appear on your Mac. Click "Accept" to answer the call in the FaceTime app. You can also choose to accept it as an audio call or send a message or reminder to call back later. Group FaceTime calls display a "Join" button to open the FaceTime app and join the call.

HANDING OFF THE CALL

With macOS Ventura or later, iOS 16 or later, and iPadOS 16 or later, you can hand off active calls to your other devices. This works similarly to handing off other tasks. Click the notification on the device you want to transfer the call to, and then click "Join" or "Switch" to complete the handoff. If you're using a Bluetooth headset, the call audio will also switch to the other device, provided that your phone number or Apple ID is selected for FaceTime in the settings on both devices.

SMS & MMS FROM YOUR MAC

To set up SMS and MMS messaging on your Mac using your iPhone, follow these steps:

1. On your iPhone, open Settings and select Messages.
2. Tap on Text Message Forwarding.
3. If you don't see the Text Message Forwarding option, ensure that you have signed into iMessage using the same Apple ID on both your iPhone and your Mac.
4. Turn on your Mac in the list of devices.
5. If you're not using two-factor authentication, you will see a six-digit activation code on your Mac. Enter this code into your iPhone when prompted and tap Allow.

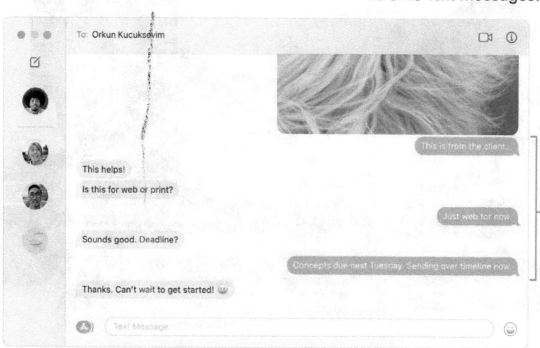

When the message bubbles are green, it means they were sent as SMS text messages.

UNLOCKING YOUR MAC WITH YOUR APPLE WATCH

Unlocking your MacBook and approving tasks with your Apple Watch is a convenient and secure way to enhance the usability of your devices. Here are the steps to set up and use these features:

1. Ensure that you are signed in to both your Mac and Apple Watch using the same Apple ID.
2. Turn on two-factor authentication for your Apple ID. You can do this by opening System Preferences, clicking your Apple ID in the sidebar, and selecting "Password & Security." Then, choose "Set Up Two-Factor Authentication."
3. Make sure the "Disable automatic login" option is selected. If you're using FileVault, you won't see this option, but you can still use the Auto Unlock feature. Set up Auto Unlock. Sign in on all your devices with the same Apple ID, then open System Preferences on your MacBook. Click "Touch ID & Password" in the sidebar, and turn on the unlock settings for Apple Watch.

Now, when you approach your sleeping MacBook wearing your authenticated Apple Watch, simply lift the cover or press a key to wake it up, and your Apple Watch will unlock it, allowing you to start working immediately.

APPROVING TASKS WITH APPLE WATCH

If you're prompted for a password, you can use your Apple Watch to authenticate on your Mac:

1. 1. Double-click the side button on your Apple Watch to authenticate your password on your Mac.

   Double-click the side button to approve requests from your Mac.

2. 2. You can use this feature to view passwords in Safari, approve app installations, unlock locked notes, and more (requires watchOS 6).

These features work seamlessly when your Apple Watch is authenticated with a passcode, and there are no extra steps required after you enter your passcode.

AIRPRINT

Printing documents and photos wirelessly without the need for printer drivers is easy with AirPrint on your Mac. Here's a simple guide on how to use AirPrint:

PRINTING WITH AIRPRINT

1. Make sure your printer is AirPrint-enabled.
2. You can print wirelessly using AirPrint to:
    - An AirPrint-enabled printer on your Wi-Fi network.
    - A network printer or a printer shared by another Mac on your Wi-Fi network.
    - A printer connected to the USB port of an AirPort base station.
3. Open the app where your document or photo is located.
4. Click on "File" and select "Print" or press Command-P to open the Print dialog.
5. In the Print dialog, click on the "Printer" pop-up menu.
6. Choose your printer from the "Nearby Printers" list.

TROUBLESHOOTING

If you can't find your printer in the Nearby Printers list, follow these steps:

1. Make sure that your printer is connected to the same Wi-Fi network as your MacBook.
2. If the printer is connected to the same network and still isn't visible, you can add it manually:
    - Open System Settings.
    - Click on "Printers & Scanners" in the sidebar.

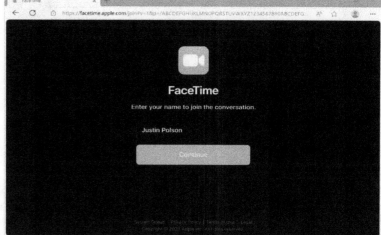

3. On the right, click on "Add Printer, Scanner, or Fax."
3. 4. If necessary, you may have to temporarily connect the printer to your MacBook using a USB cable and an adapter.

By following these steps, you can easily use AirPrint to print wirelessly from your Mac to your compatible printer.

APPS

Enjoy Apple's pre-installed apps and in-app functionalities for entertainment, seamless connections, and enhanced productivity.

App Store

Included Apps

Icon/App name	Icon/App name	Icon/App name
App Store	Books	Calendar
FaceTime	Find My	Freeform
GarageBand	Home	iMovie
Keynote	Mail	Maps
Messages	Music	News
Notes	Numbers	Pages
Photos	Podcasts	Preview
Reminders	Safari	Shortcuts
Stocks	TV	Voice Memos

Apart from the apps mentioned in the table on the left, your Mac also has other apps and utilities that could be useful. These include Calculator ⊞ Chess ▦ Clock 🕐 , Contacts 👤 TextEdit ✎ , Weather ☁ , and many more. To find these additional apps, follow these steps:

1. Open your Applications folder. You can do this by clicking on the desktop or using Finder 🙂 from your Dock, then selecting "Go" from the menu bar and choosing "Applications."

2. Inside the Applications folder, you'll find a wide range of apps and utilities, some of which may not be featured in the table mentioned earlier.

3. If you want to explore a complete list of all the apps and utilities installed on your Mac, refer to the macOS User Guide for a detailed inventory.

4. Additionally, if you're looking for more apps to enhance your Mac's capabilities, you can visit the App Store. To access the App Store, click on its icon 🅰 in your Dock. The App Store offers a vast selection of apps to fulfill almost any task you have in mind. For a comprehensive guide on how to browse and download apps from the App Store, please explore the dedicated section in the guide.

APP STORE

The App Store on your MacBook is where you can discover, download, and keep your apps up-to-date. Here's how to make the most of it:

Click a tab to browse apps.

Search for an app by name.

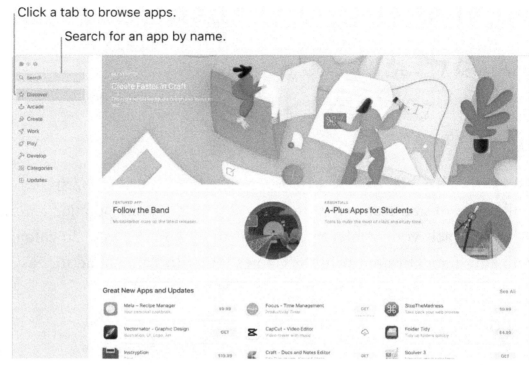

FINDING APPS

To search for a specific app, type its name in the search field and press Return. When you download an app from the App Store, it will automatically appear in Launchpad for easy access.

You can also explore new apps by selecting a tab in the sidebar, such as Create, Work, or Play, and browse through the results.

USING SIRI

If you prefer using voice commands, you can ask Siri to help you find apps. For example, you can say, "Find apps for kids."

APPLE ID

To download free apps, sign in with your Apple ID. Click "Sign In" at the bottom of the sidebar in the App Store. If you don't have an Apple ID yet, click "Create Apple ID." If you have an existing Apple ID but can't remember your password, you can recover it by clicking "Forgot Apple ID or password." You'll also need to set up an account with purchasing information to buy fee-based apps.

IPHONE AND IPAD APPS ON MAC

Many iPhone and iPad apps are compatible with your MacBook. Any apps you've previously purchased for your iPhone or iPad will appear on your Mac. Search the App Store to see if they're available for Mac.

APPLE ARCADE

Click the Arcade tab to explore Apple Arcade, a subscription service that offers a collection of games to play. You can also find games popular among your Game Center friends, track your achievements, and more. Games you download from the App Store will automatically appear in the Games folder in Launchpad for easy access.

GAME CAPTURE

For gaming enthusiasts, you can capture up to a 15-second video clip of your gameplay by pressing the share button on supported third-party game controllers. This allows you to review your strategy or keep memorable gaming moments.

APP UPDATES

You have available updates.

Keep your apps up-to-date by checking the App Store icon in the Dock. If it has a badge, it means there are updates available. Click the icon to open the App Store, then click "Updates" in the sidebar.

TOUCH BAR (ON 13-INCH MACBOOK)

If you have a 13-inch MacBook with a Touch Bar, you can use it to quickly navigate to different tabs within the App Store, such as Discover, Arcade, Create, Work, Play, Develop, Categories, and Updates.

The App Store is your one-stop-shop for all app-related needs on your MacBook, from finding new apps to keeping your current ones up-to-date.

BOOKS

If you want to buy books and audiobooks using the Books app 📖 on your Mac, it's a piece of cake.

SEARCHING

FOR BOOKS OR

AUDIOBOOKS

1. Open the Books app 📖 on your Mac.
2. Click on the search field.
3. Start typing, and you'll see suggestions. You can search by title, author, genre, or publisher.
4. Select a suggestion or press Return to perform the search.
5. To filter your results, use the options in the "Filter by" menu, or click "All" to see all results.

Type what you're looking for.

View your books and lists.

BROWSING THE STORES

1. In the Books app 📖 , you can access the Book Store or Audiobook Store from the sidebar.
2. Scroll down or click "Browse Sections" in the upper-right corner.
3. Choose a store section, such as "For You" or "Top Charts," or select a genre like "History" or "Romance."

SETTING READING GOALS

If you want to motivate yourself, set daily reading goals. By default, it's set to 5 minutes a day, but you can adjust it by clicking the "Adjust Goal" ⚙️ button in the Reading Goals section of "Reading Now." If you wish to turn off reading goals or clear reading goal data, you can do so in Books settings.

ADDING BOOKMARKS, NOTES, AND HIGHLIGHTS

To add bookmarks, notes, and highlights, move your pointer to the top of the book you're reading to show controls. Click the Add Bookmark button 🔖 to bookmark a page, and tap the bookmark again to remove it. To go to a bookmarked page, show the controls, tap 🔖 the Show Bookmarks button, and then click the bookmark 📑 .

You can also add notes and highlights by selecting the text and choosing a highlight color or "Add Note" from the pop-up menu. To access your notes later, show the controls and click the Notes and Highlights button.

SYNC ACROSS DEVICES

Your purchased books, collections, bookmarks, highlights, notes, and the current page you're reading are available automatically on your Mac, iOS devices, and iPadOS devices as long as you're signed in with the same Apple ID.

BUYING, DOWNLOADING, OR PRE-ORDERING BOOKS

1. In the Books app, go to the Book Store from the sidebar.
2. Search for or select a book you're interested in.
3. Click the book's price or the "Get" button.
4. To save a book for later, click "Want to Read." It will be added to the "Want to Read" collection in your library.
5. If available, you can also try out a book by clicking "Sample." The sample will be added to the "My Samples" collection in your library.

— Use Night theme.

NIGHT THEME

For easier reading in low-light conditions, you can change to Night theme. Simply choose View > Theme, then select "Night." However, please note that not all books support this theme.

CALENDAR

Using the Calendar app on your Mac can help you stay organized to create events, customize calendars, add holiday calendars, and filter your calendars with Focus

CREATING EVENTS

- Click the Add button ✚ or double-click anywhere in a day to create an event.
- To invite someone, double-click the event, click the "Add Invitees" section, then type their email address.
- The Calendar app will keep you informed about their responses.

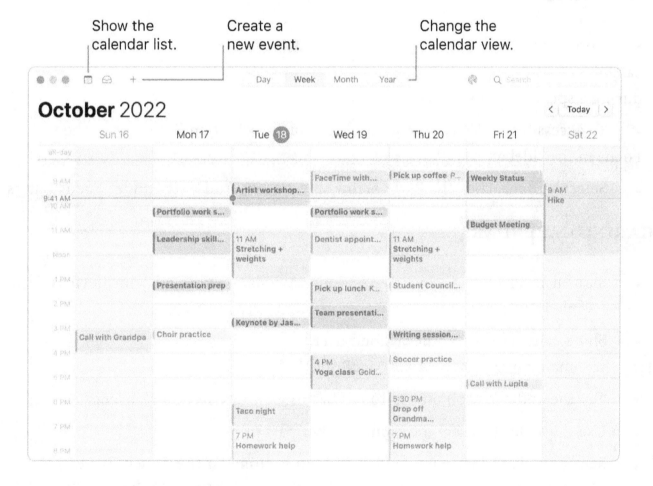

CUSTOMIZING CALENDARS

- Create separate calendars for different parts of your life by choosing File > New Calendar.
- Assign each calendar a different color by Control-clicking the calendar and choosing a new color.

ADDING HOLIDAY CALENDARS

- View holiday calendars from different regions worldwide by choosing File > New Holiday Calendar.

- Select the holiday calendar you want to add.

FILTERING CALENDARS

WITH FOCUS

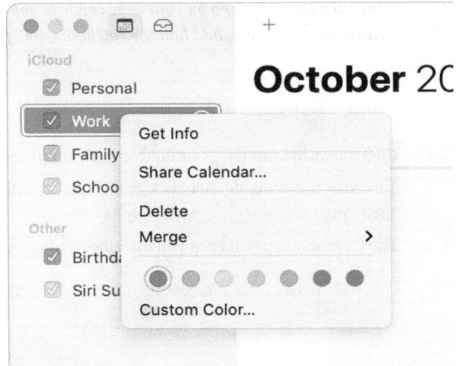

- Choose which calendars to display during a specific Focus.

- To access this feature, choose Apple Menu > System Preferences, then click Focus in the sidebar.

- Select a Focus, click the Right arrow, and choose Add Filter under Focus Filters.

SHARING CALENDARS

- Sign in to iCloud to synchronize your calendars across all your devices with the same Apple ID.

- Share calendars with other iCloud users.

Using the Touch Bar (on the 13-inch MacBook):

- Tap the Today button on the Touch Bar to view or edit today's events.

- Use the slider to select the month, either past or future.

- Select an event in your calendar and tap buttons on the Touch Bar to specify the calendar, view event details, edit time or location, and manage invitees.

By following these steps, you can efficiently manage your schedule, color-code your events, and stay on top of important dates.

FACETIME

Making video, audio, and group calls directly from your Mac is simple, all with just a few simple steps.

1. SIGN IN TO FACETIME

- Open the FaceTime app 📹 on your Mac, enter your Apple ID and password in the FaceTime window and then click "Next."

2. MAKE A CALL

- Click the "New FaceTime" button.
- Enter the phone number, email address, or name from your Contacts list for the person you want to call.
- Click the "FaceTime" button to make a video call or click ⌄ "FaceTime Audio" for an audio-only call.

3. ACCEPT OR DECLINE CALLS

When you receive a FaceTime call, you have options.
- Click "Answer" to accept the call immediately.
- Click ⌄ to accept an audio-only call.
- Click "Decline" to decline the call.
- Alternatively, message the caller or set a reminder to call them later.

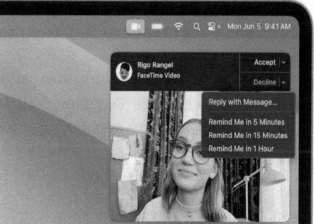

4. ADD PEOPLE TO A CALL

- Click the "Sidebar" ⊟ button.
- Click the plus button ➕ next to "Add People" for a video call.
- For an audio-only call, click the "Audio" button in the menu bar, then the arrow in the window that appears, and then "Add."

5. USE VIDEO EFFECTS

During a FaceTime video call, you can use video effects on compatible Macs to enhance your call experience. Click the "Video" button in the menu bar and choose from available video effects, such as reactions, blur your background with Portrait mode, turn on Centre Stage, and more.

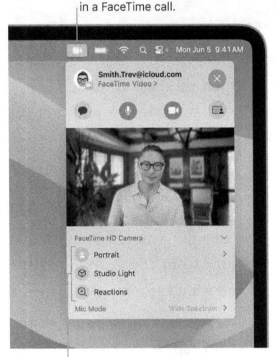

Appears when you're in a FaceTime call.

Depending on your Mac, you can adjust some or all of these video effects.

6. CREATE A FACETIME LINK (MACOS 12 OR LATER)

In the FaceTime app 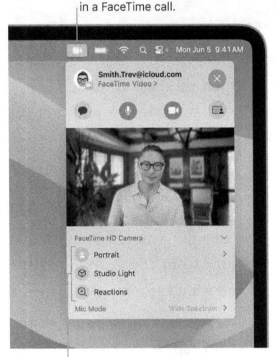, sign in to your Apple ID and click "Create Link" to generate a link for the FaceTime call.

7. START A CALL FROM A FACETIME LINK

If you created a FaceTime link, you can start the call from an app or from FaceTime itself. Double-click the FaceTime call link or find it in the list of recent calls in the "Upcoming" section. Click the "Video" button and then "Join" to start the call.

8. LET CALLERS JOIN THE FACETIME CALL

As the originator of the FaceTime link, you can allow others to join the call immediately. When a new caller is waiting, you'll see a badge on the "Sidebar" button. Click the "Sidebar" button and choose to "Allow the caller to join the call" or "Don't allow the caller to join the call."

9. DELETE A FACETIME LINK

To delete a FaceTime link you created, you can delete it. Check the list of callers for the call made with a FaceTime link, click the "Info" button, and select "Delete Link."

FIND MY APP

Find My is a helpful app that enables you to locate your friends, family, and Apple devices.

SHARE LOCATIONS WITH FRIENDS

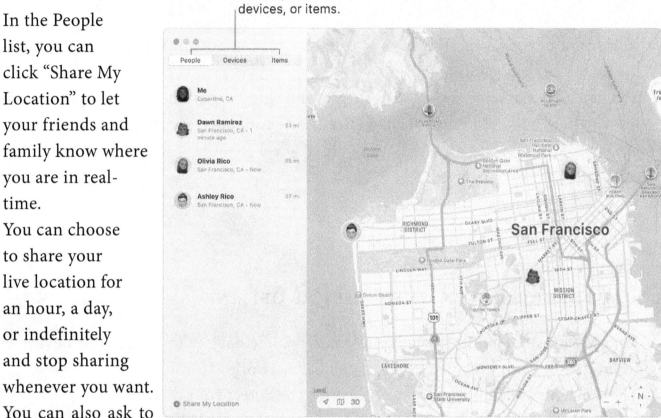

- In the People list, you can click "Share My Location" to let your friends and family know where you are in real-time.
- You can choose to share your live location for an hour, a day, or indefinitely and stop sharing whenever you want.
- You can also ask to follow a friend, allowing you to see their location on a map and receive step-by-step directions to their whereabouts.

SET LOCATION ALERTS

- You can configure location alerts to notify your friends when you arrive at or leave a specific location.
- You can also receive notifications when your friends arrive or leave particular places.
- If your friends create notifications about your location, you can find them all in one place by clicking "Me" in the People list and scrolling to "Notifications About You."

GET NOTIFIED WHEN YOU LEAVE SOMETHING BEHIND

- To avoid leaving your devices, such as your MacBook, behind, you can set up separation alerts on your iPhone, iPad, or iPod touch.

- These alerts will notify you when you move away from your device.
- To set up separation alerts for a device, click the Info icon for that device and select "Notify When Left Behind." Follow the onscreen instructions.

SECURE A LOST DEVICE

- Find My allows you to locate and protect lost devices, such as your Mac, iPhone, or AirPods.
- Click on a device in the Devices list to locate it on the map. You can play a sound on the device to help you find it.
- You can also mark the device as lost, preventing others from accessing your personal information, and even erase the device remotely for added security.

LOCATE DEVICES, EVEN WHEN THEY'RE OFFLINE

- Find My uses Bluetooth signals from nearby Apple devices to locate your device, even when it's not connected to a Wi-Fi or cellular network.
- These signals are anonymous and encrypted to protect your privacy.
- You can even locate a device that has been erased, provided it meets the compatibility requirements.

FIND EVERYDAY ITEMS

- You can attach an AirTag to items like your keychain to find them quickly when they go missing.
- Use your iOS or iPadOS device to register an AirTag and compatible third-party items to your Apple ID. In Find My on your Mac, you can click the "Items" tab to view the location of your items on a map.

If an item can't be located, you can check its last known location and receive a notification when it's found. You can also activate Lost Mode for an item, including a custom message and contact number for recovery.

FREE FORM

Freeform is a powerful and versatile tool that allows you to organize your ideas and collaborate with others on macOS Ventura 13.1 or later.

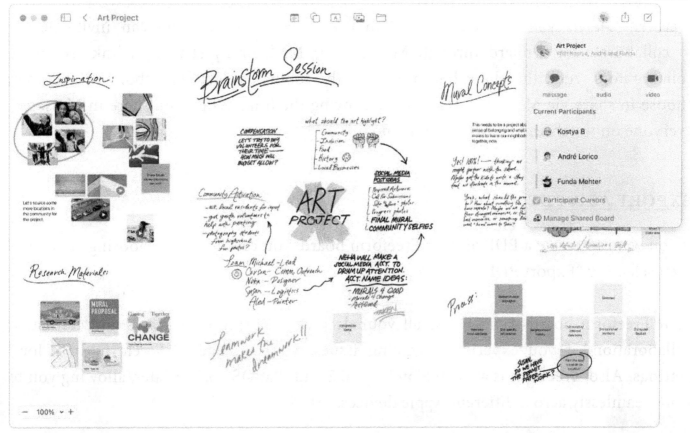

CREATE A BOARD

To create a new board, simply click the "New Board" button located in the toolbar. You don't need to worry about saving your board as it is done automatically. To give your board a name, click on "Untitled" in the top left of the title bar and enter the desired name.

ADD CONTENT

Use the toolbar to insert different types of elements into your board such as text, sticky notes, photos, links, and files. You can also drag items from other apps onto your board.

ORGANIZE YOUR BOARD

Freeform provides tools for arranging and managing items on your board. You can move, resize, group, and align items as needed. You can also choose to view your board with a grid or use alignment guides to help you position items accurately.

COLLABORATION

Freeform allows you to collaborate with others in real-time. You can invite people to collaborate on a board through Messages or Mail, or by sharing a link. To invite collaborators, click the share button ⬆️ in the toolbar, select "Collaborate," and then choose to share via Messages, Mail, or by copying the link. When you share in Messages, everyone on the thread is invited to the board.

EXPORT AS A PDF

If you want to create a PDF of your Freeform board, you can do so by choosing "File" and then selecting "Export PDF."

Your Freeform boards sync across all your devices, ensuring easy access and consistent collaboration. If you experience syncing issues, you can enable Freeform in iCloud Settings. Also, Freeform is available on iOS 16.2 and iPadOS 16.2 or later, allowing you to work seamlessly across different Apple devices.

GARAGEBAND

GarageBand is an amazing application that allows you to create, record, and share your music. Whether you are an aspiring musician or a seasoned artist, unleash your creativity and build your own home recording studio.

CREATE A NEW PROJECT

- Start by creating a new project. You can either begin from scratch or use a pre-made song template.

- Customize your project by selecting the tempo, key, and other options that suit your music style. Tap the ❓ button if you need any help with how items work.

- Click "Record" to start playing and building your song. GarageBand offers various tracks and loops to help you craft your musical masterpiece.

ADD INSTRUMENTS AND LOOPS

- Quickly enhance your project with drums and other instruments using Loops.
- Click the "Loop Browser" ⬭ to explore a vast collection of loops categorized by instrument, genre, or descriptor.
- Drag and drop the desired loop into an empty section of the Tracks area.
- You can customize loops to seamlessly blend with your composition using straightforward controls.

RECORD YOUR VOICE

- To record your voice, go to "Track" and choose "New Track."
- Select the microphone under "Audio."
- Click the triangle next to "Details" to set various options for input, output, and monitoring.
- Click "Create" to confirm the settings.
- Hit the "Record" button ● to begin recording your voice, and press the "Play" button ▶ to stop the recording.

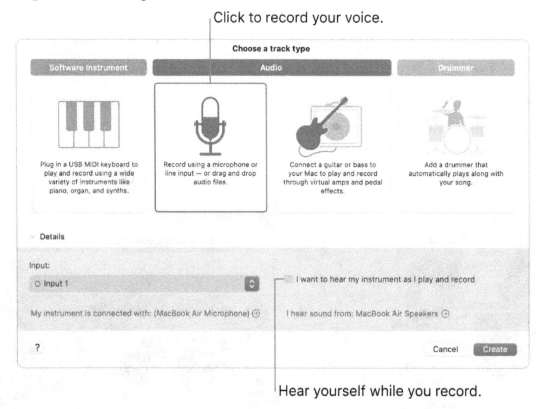

Click to record your voice.

Hear yourself while you record.

SMART CONTROLS AND EFFECTS

- Take advantage of the Touch Bar on your 13-inch MacBook to fine-tune the sound of your selected track.
- Easily adjust Smart Controls to modify the instrument's sound, enable or disable effects, or adjust track volume.

GarageBand is an excellent platform for musicians of all levels to express their creativity and bring their musical ideas to life. Whether you're a singer, instrumentalist, or music producer, GarageBand offers a user-friendly and feature-rich environment for music creation.

HOME

Control your home accessories, safely, with your MAC!

Siri can help you control your smart home accessories using your Mac. Besides setting reminders and answering questions, Siri is here to make your life more convenient by allowing you to control your home devices. This chapter explores how you can use the home app 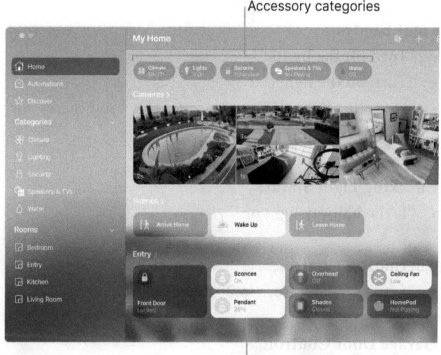 to control your accessories and scenes with Siri on your Mac.

The Home app on your Mac provides a whole-house view, allowing you to see your entire home at a glance, including cameras, scenes, and accessories organized by room. You can easily control your HomeKit accessories, from lights to thermostats, securely using your Mac.

Accessory categories

Click an accessory to control it.

Accessory Control

The Home app offers accessory control through tiles with icons, making it intuitive to interact with your devices. You can turn lights on or off, lock or unlock doors, open or close blinds, and more. Adjusting brightness and temperature is also a breeze.

Categories

Categories such as Lights, Climate, Security, Speakers & TVs, and Water help you quickly access relevant accessories organized by room, along with detailed status information.

Scenes

Create scenes in the Home app to make multiple accessories work together with a single command. For example, you can create a "Good Night" scene that turns off all lights, closes shades, and locks the door when it's time for bed.

Home Security Cameras

With the ability to view your cameras and HomeKit Secure Video, you can connect your home security cameras to record footage and view it securely from anywhere. Up to nine camera views are displayed in the Home tab, end-to-end encrypted.

Adaptive Lighting

Adaptive lighting is another feature, allowing you to set smart light bulbs to adjust the color temperature throughout the day to enhance comfort and productivity.

USING SIRI:

Light Control:

- "Turn off the lights."
- "Turn on the lights."
- "Dim the lights." Then specify the brightness, for example, "Set brightness to 55 percent."

Checking Light Status:

- "Is the hallway light on?"

Thermostat Control:

- "Set the temperature to 20 degrees."

Garage Door Control:

- "Close the garage door."

Room and Scene Control:

If you've set up rooms or scenes, you can use commands like "I'm home" or "I'm leaving."

- "Turn down the kitchen lights."
- "Turn on the fan in the office."
- "Set my reading scene."

It's important to note that Siri can work with some third-party accessories as well. If prompted, you can set up these accessories and control their settings using Siri.

EMAILS

Apple's Mail 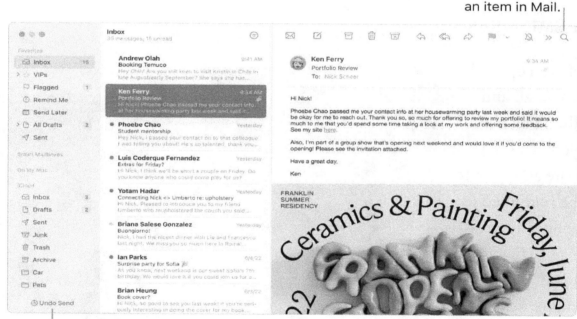 *is a powerful tool for managing your email accounts efficiently. It supports popular email services like iCloud, Gmail, Yahoo Mail, and AOL Mail, allowing you to consolidate all your emails in one place on your Mac.*

ONE-STOP EMAIL

Instead of logging into multiple websites to check your email accounts, you can set up all your email accounts in the Mail app. This way, you can access all your messages in one convenient location. To add an account, go to Mail > Add Account.

SIRI INTEGRATION

You can use Siri to compose and send emails effortlessly. For example, you can say, "Email Laura about the trip," and Siri will help you draft the message.

SMART SEARCH

The Mail app features a smart search that provides accurate results, corrects typos, and even suggests synonyms for your search terms. This makes it easier to find the messages you're looking for. Smart search also offers a richer view of shared content as you search for email messages.

Click to search for an item in Mail.

Click to Undo Send.

MESSAGE MANAGEMENT

Keep your inbox organized by blocking messages from specific senders, moving their emails to the Trash. You can also mute overly active email threads and unsubscribe from mailing lists directly within the Mail app.

SCHEDULED SENDING

You can schedule your emails to be sent at the perfect time. When composing a message, click the dropdown menu next to the Send button and select a suggested time or choose "Send Later" to set a specific date and time.

UNDO SEND

If you accidentally send an email before it's ready, you can easily unsend it within 10 seconds after sending. Customize the time frame for undoing sends by going to Mail Settings > Composing.

EFFICIENCY AND ORGANIZATION

Mail helps you stay efficient and organized. It notifies you when you forget to include important parts of your message, like a recipient. Sent email messages that don't receive a response are intelligently moved to the top of your inbox for easy follow-up.

REMINDERS

If you opened an email and didn't respond, you can set a date and time to be reminded to follow up. Just right-click the email in your inbox, select "Remind Me," and choose when you'd like to be reminded.

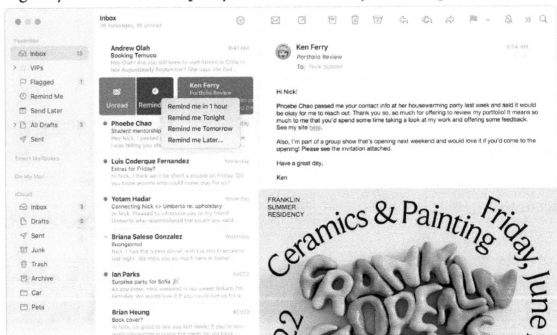

You have unread messages.

EVENTS AND CONTACTS

INTEGRATION

Add events and contacts directly from emails. If you receive a message containing a new

89

email address or event, you can click "Add" within the message to add it to Contacts or Calendar.

PRIVACY PROTECTION

Protect your privacy with the Privacy Protection feature, which hides your IP address from email senders. It also prevents senders from knowing if you've opened their emails. Turn this feature on in Mail Settings > Privacy.

HIDE MY EMAIL

With an iCloud+ subscription, you can create unique, random email addresses for added privacy when interacting with websites. This feature allows you to send and receive messages without sharing your real email address. You can create, manage, or disable Hide My Email addresses in iCloud settings.

TRANSLATION

Translate text quickly by selecting the text, right-clicking it, and choosing "Translate." You can also download languages to work offline. on your Mac, choose Apple Menu > System Settings, then click General in the sideba

PERSONALIZATION

Add emoji, photos, or sketches to your messages with ease. You can insert photos from your library or take new ones using your iPhone or iPad. Continuity Camera lets you insert photos and sketches from other devices.

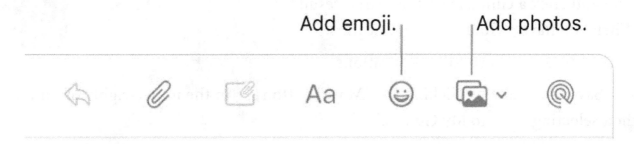

Add emoji.   Add photos.

FULL SCREEN MODE

When using Mail in full screen, new message windows open in Split View on the right, making it easy to reference other messages in your inbox as you write.

MAPS

Maps on your Mac provides a great way to explore and organize places using curated Guides and your own custom Guides. If you're planning a trip or just want to discover new places, you can use Food and Travel Guides in Maps.

EXPLORE PLACES WITH GUIDES

1. Launch ⬡ Maps app on your Mac.

2. In the search field, you can:

   • Click a Guide that appears under "Guides We Love."

   • Click "See All" and choose a Guide.

   • Scroll down and click a publisher, then select a Guide.

   • Enter a word or phrase in the search field and click a Guide from the search results.

3. When you have a Guide open, you can:

   • Scroll up or down to view locations.

   • Save the Guide by clicking the "More" button ⋯ in the upper-right corner and then selecting "Add to My Guides."

   • Add a location to one of your Guides by clicking the "Add" button ⊕ next to the location and selecting a Guide. If you don't have any Guides, you can create one first.

   • See other Guides from the same publisher by clicking the "More" button and then selecting "See Publisher's Guides." If the publisher has no other guides, you can click "Publisher's Website" to visit their website.

   • See Guides for a specific location by clicking the "More" button ⋯, selecting "See

All Guides," clicking "Editors' Picks," and then choosing a location from the menu.

• Share the Guide by clicking the "Share" button under the guide's title and selecting an option.

• Explore related media by clicking links to find relevant music, books, and more.

• Close the Guide by clicking the "Close" button .

CREATE YOUR OWN GUIDE

1. Launch the Maps app on your Mac.
2. Click the "New" button in the toolbar.
3. Choose "Create New Guide."
4. Enter a name for your Guide and press Return.

ADD A PLACE TO YOUR GUIDE

1. Click a location on the map.
2. In the place card, click the Add button and select one of your Guides.

You can also click the "New" button in the toolbar, choose "Add New Place To," select a guide, and search for a location to add.

EDIT YOUR GUIDE

1. In the Maps app on your Mac, go to "My Guides" in the sidebar.
2. If your Guides aren't visible, click the arrow to reveal them.
3. To perform various actions on your Guide, you can:

• Rename the Guide by control-clicking it, choosing "Edit Guide," and entering a new name.

• Change the Guide cover photo by control-clicking it, selecting "Edit Guide," and choosing "Change Key Photo."

• Delete the Guide by tapping and control-clicking it and choosing "Delete Guide."

• Remove a place from the Guide by moving the pointer over the Guide, clicking the arrow , control-clicking the place, and selecting "Remove from Guide."

• Change the sort order by moving the pointer over the Guide, clicking the arrow, clicking the "Sort Order" button, and choosing "Name," "Distance," or "Date Added."

• Move a place to another Guide by moving the pointer over the Guide, clicking the arrow , control-clicking the place, and choosing "Move t :hen selecting another Guide.

SHARE YOUR GUIDE

1. In the Maps app 🗺 on your Mac, go to "My Guides" in the sidebar.
2. If your Guides aren't visible, click the arrow ❯ to reveal them.
3. Control-click the Guide you want to share, choose "Share," and then select an option.

Your Guides are automatically updated when new places are added, ensuring that you always have access to the latest recommendations for your food and travel adventures.

GET DIRECTIONS IN MAPS

ON MAC

If you need to navigate your way around a new place, you can easily get directions in Maps on your Mac for driving, walking, public transport, or cycling. Moreover, you can even send the directions to your iPhone, iPad, or Apple Watch for convenient access while on the go.

Click to see directions for an alternative route.

Drag to reorder the locations.

Click a step to zoom in on it.

Here's how to use the Maps app for directions:

1. Open the Maps app 🗺 on your Mac.
2. There are several ways to get directions:

    •   Click the "Directions" button ↱ in the toolbar, then enter your starting location and destination.

    •   Click on your destination on the map, such as a landmark or pin, and in the place card, click "Directions."

    •   If Maps displays your current location, it will use it as your starting point. You can drag the "Reorder" button ≡ next to a location to swap your starting and ending points.

3. Click the appropriate button to choose the mode of transportation: "Drive,"   "Walk,"
   "Public Transport,"   or "Cycle"   .
4. To view the directions list, click the "Trip Details" button   next to a route.

If you're driving, directions may include additional features like electric vehicle routing, congestion zones, and number plate restrictions in specific regions.

GET DIRECTIONS TO MULTIPLE STOPS WHEN DRIVING

1. Open the Maps app   on your Mac.
2. Click the "Directions" button   in the toolbar, then enter your starting location and destination.
3. Click the "Drive" button   .
4. Click "Add stop," then select a recently searched location or search for a location and click the result.
5. Repeat the process to add more stops as needed.
6. You can manage the stops by changing their order   , updating a stop, or deleting a stop   .

AUTOMATICALLY GET DIRECTIONS ON YOUR IPHONE OR IPAD

If you want to open the route you've searched for on your Mac in the Maps app   on your iPhone or iPad, follow these steps:
1. Open the Maps app   on your iPhone or iPad.
2. Scroll down in the search card to "Recent," then tap the route.

SEND DIRECTIONS TO YOUR IPHONE, IPAD, OR APPLE WATCH

1. In the Maps app on your Mac, select a location on the map, and click "Directions."
2. Make any necessary adjustments.
3. Click the "Share" button   in the toolbar.
4. Choose the device to which you want to send the directions.

To easily share and access directions across your Apple devices, ensure you sign in using the same Apple ID on both your Mac and your device.

LOOK AROUND IN MAPS ON MAC

1. Open the Maps app ![icon] on your Mac.
2. In the search field, enter an address, intersection, landmark, or business.
3. If available, you can click on "Look Around" below the location in the search results, select a location and then click on the "Look Around" button in the toolbar or click on the image with the "Look Around" button in the lower-left corner of the place card.

While Using Look Around, you can:

-   Drag the image left or right to look around (Pan).

-   Click in front of you in the Look Around view to move forward (Move Forward).

-   Pinch two fingers open to zoom in or close them to zoom out (Zoom In or Out).

-   Click on another location on the map to explore a different area (View Another Point of Interest).

-   Click the "Enter Full Screen" button to view the location in full screen. To exit full screen, click the "Exit Full Screen" button.

-   Click the "Close" button (×) to exit the Look Around view when you're done.

MESSAGES

Sending messages on your Mac is a convenient way to communicate with others. Below is a detailed guide on how to send messages on your Mac using the Messages app 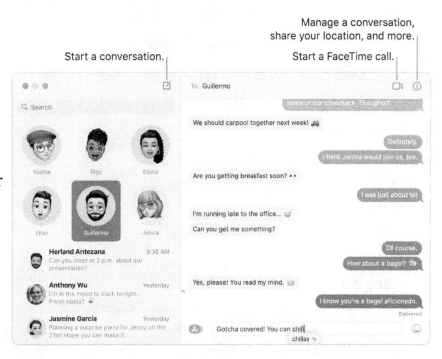.

1. Open the Messages App

   • First, locate and open the Messages app on your Mac.

2. Compose a New Message:

   • Click the "Compose" button (icon with a pencil) located in the top-right corner or use the Touch Bar if your Mac supports it.

3. Choose Recipient

   • Type the name, email address, or phone number of the person you want to send a message to in the "To" field. As you type, Messages will suggest matching addresses from your Contacts or previous conversations.

   • Alternatively, click the "Add" button located to the right of the "To" field, select a contact from the list, and click on their email address or phone number.

4. Compose Message

   • Type your message in the field located at the bottom of the window. You can use typing suggestions if available.

5. Send Message

   • Press the "Return" key

96

on your keyboard or click the "Send" button to send the message.

6. Additional Features

- Messages on Mac offers various features to enhance your messages, such as Tapbacks, sending photos, videos, stickers, audio messages, and using message effects. You can use these options to make your messages more engaging.

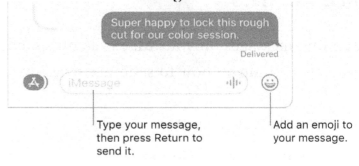

Super happy to lock this rough cut for our color session.

Delivered

Type your message, then press Return to send it.

Add an emoji to your message.

7. Managing Conversations

- Messages on Mac keeps track of your conversations in the sidebar. You can easily switch between different conversations and manage your messages.

When the message bubbles are green, it means they were sent as SMS text messages.

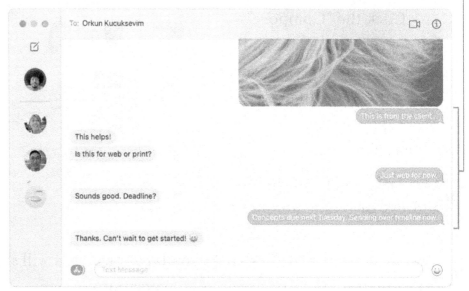

8. Using Siri

- If you prefer voice commands, you can use Siri to send messages. Just say something like, "Message Mum that I'll be late."

Please note that to send SMS and MMS messages on your Mac, your iPhone must have iOS 8.1 or later, and both your iPhone and Mac must be signed into iMessage using the same Apple ID. This allows you to receive and send text and multimedia messages on your Mac.

If you want to make FaceTime video calls using Messages on your Mac, you can do

Click to hide the call window.

Picture-in-picture window

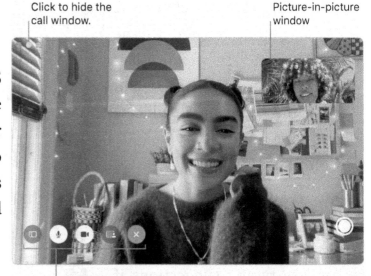

Move the pointer over FaceTime to see call options.

so by selecting a conversation, sending a message to a person or group, and clicking the "Video" button to initiate a FaceTime Video call with the selected contacts.

The Messages app  on your Mac is equipped with a helpful feature called "Shared with You" that allows you to keep track of all the content that others have shared with you in your messages. You can access this content in various apps, and this is how you can make the most of it:

TURN SHARED WITH YOU SETTINGS ON OR OFF FOR ALL APPS

1. Open the Messages app ⬭ on your Mac.
2. Go to Messages > Settings, then click "Shared with You."
3. Choose one of the following options:
   - To enable Shared with You for all apps, click "Turn On."
   - To disable Shared with You for all apps, click "Turn Off."

TURN SHARED WITH YOU ON OR OFF BY CONVERSATION

1. In the Messages app ⬭ on your Mac, select a conversation.
2. Click the "Info" button ⓘ in the top-right corner of the conversation.
3. Select "Show in Shared with You" to enable shared content to appear in the corresponding app's Shared with You section. Deselect this option to remove shared content from the Shared with You section.

SHARE CONTENT WITH OTHERS

1. Select the content you want to share, such as a link, and click the "Share" button ⬆ or choose "Share."
2. Choose "Messages."

3. In the "To" field, type the name, email address, or phone number of the person you want to send the content to. Messages will suggest matching addresses from your Contacts or previous conversations as you type.
4. Enter a message if desired.
5. Click "Send."

VIEW SHARED CONTENT

You can view the content that others have shared with you either in your Messages conversation or later in the corresponding apps. The Shared with You section is available in various apps, including Apple TV, Books, Finder, Freeform (macOS 13.1 or later), News, Notes, Photos, Podcasts, Reminders, Safari, iWork apps, and some third-party apps.

For example, to view shared content in the Apple TV app ⏵tv, click "Watch Now," then scroll down to the "Shared with You" row.

CONTINUE THE CONVERSATION

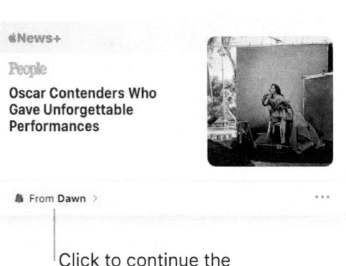

In the corresponding apps, shared content includes a button with the name of the person who sent it. You can click this button to continue the conversation about the shared content. For example, in the News app 📰 , click the "From" label to send a reply in Messages.

PIN SHARED CONTENT

If you find shared content particularly interesting, you can pin it in Messages, and it will be highlighted in Shared with You, Messages search, and the Info view of the conversation.

1. In the Messages app ⬤ on your Mac, select a conversation.
2. Control-click the shared content, then choose "Pin."

This way, you can easily keep track of the content shared with you and access it when it's convenient for you in various apps.

MUSIC

If you want to access a vast library of songs, listen to music offline, create playlists, and enjoy various features, subscribing to Apple Music on your Mac is an excellent option.

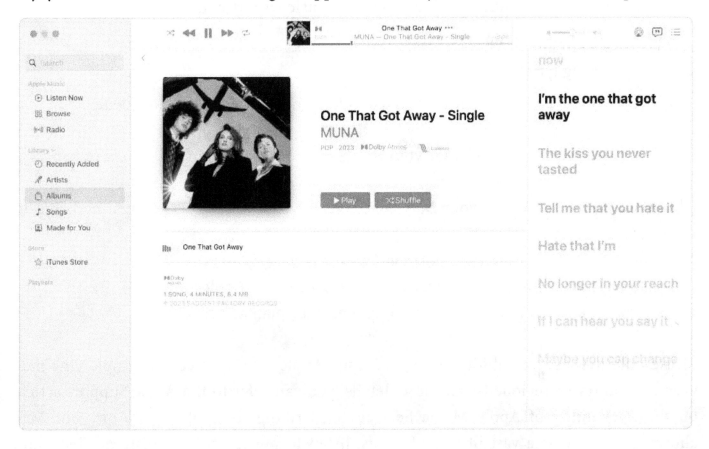

SUBSCRIBE TO APPLE MUSIC ON YOUR MAC

1. Open the Music app 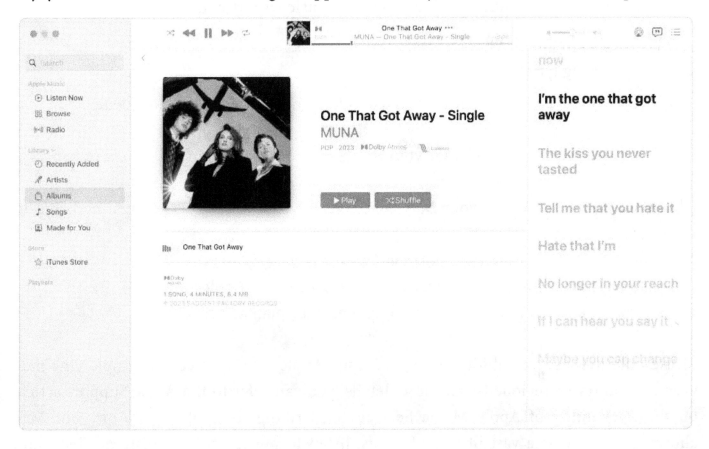 on your Mac.
2. In the menu bar, go to "Account" and select "Join Apple Music."
3. Follow the on-screen instructions.
4. If prompted, sign in with your Apple ID. If you don't have an Apple ID, you can create one during the setup.

Once you become an Apple Music subscriber, you can enjoy the following benefits:

• Stream recommended songs on up to 10 computers and devices.

• Select artists as favorites to receive notifications about them and easily find their music.

• Download songs for offline listening.

• Access your music library on all your devices.

- Play Apple Music radio stations.

- Listen to music together using SharePlay on a FaceTime call.

- Listen to and download songs in lossless audio and Dolby Atmos (spatial) audio.

- Create an Apple Music profile and share music with friends.

- Allow third-party apps to access Apple Music.

- View song lyrics.

- Use Autoplay to automatically add similar songs to the end of the queue.

If you ever need to cancel or change your Apple Music subscription, follow these steps:

1. In the Music app 🎵 on your Mac, go to "Account" > "Account Settings" and sign in with your Apple ID.
2. In the "Settings" section, click "Manage" next to Subscriptions.
3. Click "Edit" next to Apple Music, Apple Music Voice, or Apple One.
4. Choose to cancel your subscription or change your plan as needed.

Please note that the availability of Apple Music, Apple Music Voice, and Apple One may vary by country or region. To get more details, you can refer to the Apple Support article on the Availability of Apple Media Services.Subscribing to Apple Music on your Mac allows you to access a vast library of songs, listen to music offline, create playlists, and enjoy various features. Here's how to subscribe to Apple Music on your Mac:

SUBSCRIBE TO APPLE MUSIC

1. Open the Music app 🎵 on your Mac.
2. In the menu bar, go to "Account" and select "Join Apple Music."
3. Follow the onscreen instructions.
4. If prompted, sign in with your Apple ID. If you don't have an Apple ID, you can create one during the setup.

ABOUT YOUR APPLE MUSIC SUBSCRIPTION

Once you become an Apple Music subscriber, you can enjoy the following benefits:
Stream recommended songs on up to 10 computers and devices.
Select artists as favorites to receive notifications about them and easily find their music.
Download songs for offline listening.

ACCESS YOUR MUSIC LIBRARY ON ALL YOUR DEVICES

- Play Apple Music radio stations.
- Listen to music together using SharePlay on a FaceTime call.
- Listen to and download songs in lossless audio and Dolby Atmos (spatial) audio.
- Create an Apple Music profile and share music with friends.
- Allow third-party apps to access Apple Music.
- View song lyrics.
- Use Autoplay to automatically add similar songs to the end of the queue.

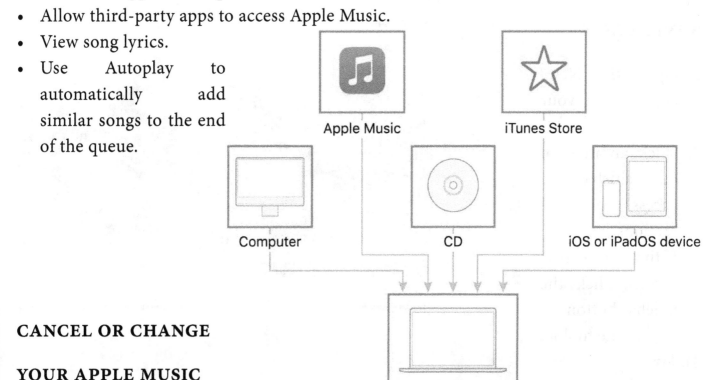

Apple Music   iTunes Store

Computer   CD   iOS or iPadOS device

Your music library

CANCEL OR CHANGE YOUR APPLE MUSIC SUBSCRIPTION

If you ever need to cancel or change your Apple Music subscription, follow these steps:

1. In the Music app 🎵 on your Mac, go to "Account" > "Account Settings" and sign in with your Apple ID.
2. In the "Settings" section, click "Manage" next to Subscriptions.
3. Click "Edit" next to Apple Music, Apple Music Voice, or Apple One.
4. Choose to cancel your subscription or change your plan as needed.
5. Please note that Apple Music, Apple Music Voice, and Apple One availability may vary by country or region. To get more details, you can refer to the Apple Support article on the Availability of Apple Media Services.

NEWS

Apple News on your Mac provides a wide array of channels, topics, and stories to explore.

SIDEBAR

NAVIGATION

1. Open the News app 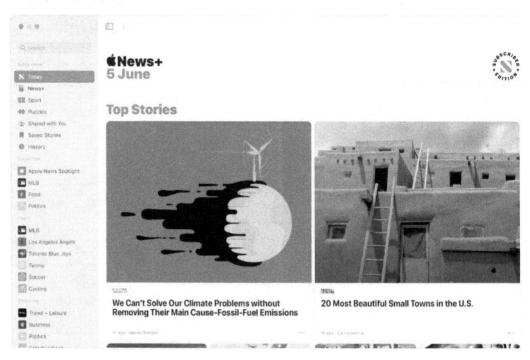 on your Mac.
2. Click an item in the sidebar to access different sections.
- If the sidebar isn't shown, click the Sidebar button ▭ in the toolbar.

Today

- Features top stories selected by Apple News editors.

- Displays stories from the channels and topics you follow.

- In some regions, it includes personalized local news and weather reports based on your location.

- If you're an Apple News+ subscriber, My Magazines shows issues from magazines you follow.

News+

- Provides access to hundreds of magazines, popular newspapers, and other publications available through Apple News+.

- Subscribers can browse recent issues, download them, and read publications.

Puzzles

- Exclusive to Apple News+ subscribers, where you can solve daily crossword and crossword mini puzzles.

Shared with You

- Shows stories shared with you by others via the Messages app .

- Conveniently aggregates shared stories in one location.

Sport

- Allows you to follow your favorite sports, leagues, teams, and athletes.

- Receive stories from top sporting publications, local newspapers, and more.

- Access scores, fixtures, standings for professional and college leagues.

- Watch highlights.

Favourites

- Lists the channels and topics you've marked as your favorites.

- You can customize this list at any time.

- You may already have some channels and topics that were automatically added to Favourites.

Suggested

- Lists channels and topics suggested by Siri or based on your interactions within Apple News.

- May include local news suggestions in some regions based on your location.

Search and Discover Channels

- If a specific channel or topic isn't shown, use the search field at the top of the sidebar to search within Apple News.

- You can also choose "File" > "Discover Channels" to explore more content.

WHILE READING A STORY

- Watch videos, ask for more or fewer stories like it, share it, or save it for later.

- Navigate to the next or previous story using the arrow keys.
- Access the story's channel by clicking the Share button in the toolbar and choosing "Go to Channel."

FOLLOW CHANNELS OR TOPICS

1. Open the News app 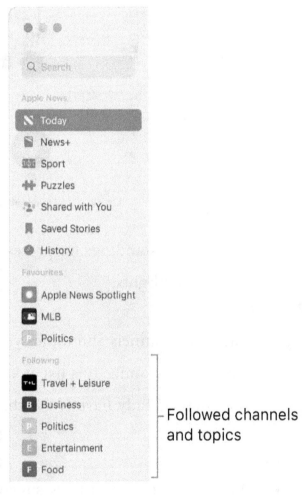 on your Mac.
2. To follow channels or topics, you can:

- Choose "File" > "Discover Channels," select the channels you want to follow by the + icon should change to ✅, and click "Done."

- In ⊕ Today feed, click the "Add" button next to a channel or topic, or click the More button ⋯ and choose "Follow Channel" or "Follow Topic."

- While viewing stories for a specific topic or channel, choose "File" > "Follow Topic" or "Follow Channel."

- If you're reading a story, choose "File" > "Follow Channel" or click the Share button 🔼 in the toolbar and select "Follow Channel."

- If the channel, topic, or story you want to follow isn't shown, you can search for it in Apple News and follow it from the search results.

UNFOLLOW CHANNELS OR TOPICS

To unfollow a channel or topic, do the following:

- In the sidebar (if not shown, click the Sidebar button ▭ in the toolbar), select the channel or topic, swipe with two fingers (on a trackpad) or one finger (on a mouse), then click "Unfollow."

- Choose "File" > "Unfollow Channel" or "File" > "Unfollow Topic."

- If you're reading a story from a channel you want to unfollow, choose "File" > "Unfollow Channel" or click the Share button in the toolbar and select "Unfollow Channel."

MANAGE YOUR FAVOURITES

- The "Favourites" section displays the channels and topics from your Following list that you like the most. You can customize this list at any time.

- To add a channel or topic to your Favourites, go to "Following," Control-click the channel or topic, and click "Add to Favourites."

- To remove a channel or topic from your Favourites, go to "Favourites," Control-click the channel or topic, and click "Remove from Favourites."

- You can also rearrange the items you follow in the sidebar by dragging an item below "Favourites" or "Following" to a different position.

SAVE STORIES

1. In the News app ◣ on your Mac, to save a story, you can:

- In the Today feed, click the ellipsis ••• for a story, then choose "Save Story."

- While reading a story, click the "Save" 🔖 button in the toolbar, or press Command-S.

VIEW SAVED STORIES

1. Open the News app ◣ on your Mac.
2. In the sidebar (if not shown, click the Sidebar button ▯ in the toolbar), click "Saved Stories."
3. You will see a list of saved stories.
4. Click on a saved story to view it.
5. To return to the list of saved stories, click the "Back" ‹ button in the toolbar.

UNSAVE STORIES

1. To unsave a story, view the saved story in the News app ◣ on your Mac.
2. Click the "Save" ▮ button in the toolbar, or press Command-S.

By saving stories, you can easily access and read them later, even without an internet connection. This feature allows you to catch up on articles of interest at your convenience.

NOTES

Notes app 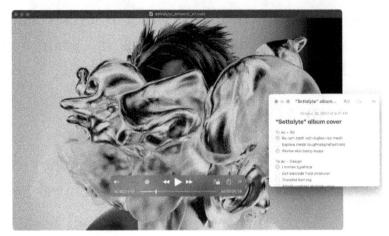 is an efficient and versatile application that provides a great platform for jotting down quick thoughts or saving longer notes with checklists, images, web links, and more. It offers a wide range of features to enhance your note-taking experience, such as:

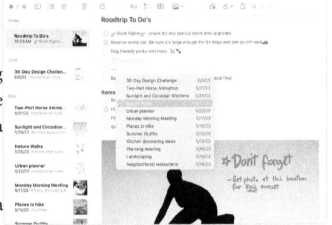

Collaboration Features

You can collaborate with others by sharing notes and folders. This allows multiple people to work on and update a note, making it a valuable tool for team projects.

Mentions

You can mention specific individuals in a note, making it easy to direct their attention to specific content within the note. This is particularly useful for communication and task assignment.

Tags

Tags help you categorize and organize your notes. You can assign tags to notes based on topics, projects, or any other criteria that make sense to you. This enhances your ability to find and manage your notes effectively.

Smart Folders

Smart Folders are a convenient way to automatically arrange your notes based on specific criteria, such as whether a note contains checklists or attachments, or when the note was created or last edited. This helps you keep your notes organized and easy to access.

iCloud Sync

With iCloud integration, your notes are seamlessly synchronized across all your Apple devices. This means you can access your notes from any device where you're signed in with your Apple ID, ensuring that your important information is always at your fingertips.

Siri Integration

You can use Siri voice commands to create a new note quickly. Just say something like, "Create a new note," and Siri will assist you in setting up a new note.

START A QUICK NOTE

If you want to start a fresh Quick Note each time instead of reopening the previous one, you can make this change by going to "Notes" > "Settings" and unselecting "Always resume to last Quick Note."

If you're working in another app and want to create a Quick Note, you have a few options:

- Keyboard Shortcut: Press and hold the Fn key or Globe key and then press Q.

- Hot Corners: Move your mouse pointer to the bottom-right corner of the screen (the default hot corner for Quick Note) and click the note that appears. You can customize or turn off this hot corner in your Mac's settings.

Adding Safari Links to a Quick Note
1. In the Safari app on your Mac, open the webpage you want to link to.
2. Click the "Share" button and choose either "New Quick Note" or "Add to Quick Note."
3. When you return to the linked content on the webpage, a thumbnail of the Quick Note will appear in the corner of the screen as a reminder of what you noted earlier.

Adding Content from Safari to a Quick Note
1. In the Safari app on your Mac, open a web page and select the text you want to add to a Quick Note.
2. Control-click the selected text, then choose "New Quick Note" or "Add to Quick Note."
3. A link will appear in the Quick Note, and the text in Safari will be highlighted. The highlighted text remains when you revisit the webpage later.

CLOSING AND REOPENING QUICK NOTES

- To close a Quick Note, click the red "Close" button located in the top left corner of the note.
- To reopen a Quick Note, use any of the methods mentioned above.

MANAGING NOTES

Managing your accounts and enhancing your note-taking experience in the Notes app on your Mac can be made easier by adding, temporarily stopping, or removing accounts. Here are the steps to perform these actions:

ADDING AN ACCOUNT

1. Open the Notes app   on your Mac.
2. In the app's menu, go to "Notes" and select "Accounts."
3. Click on "Add Account." You have the option to add various account types, including iCloud, Google, Yahoo, and others.
4. Follow the onscreen instructions to enter your account information and sign in. If you use Safari to sign in, you may need to return to the settings window to complete the process.
5. Ensure that the "Notes" option is selected for the account.
6. Click "Done" to finish the account setup.

Each account you add will be listed separately. To keep your notes synchronized across all your Apple devices, remember to set up your iPhone, iPad, and iPod touch with the same notes accounts.

TEMPORARILY STOPPING AN ACCOUNT

1. In the Notes app   on your Mac, click on "Notes" in the menu.
2. Select "Accounts."
3. Choose the account you want to temporarily stop using.
4. Turn off "Notes" for that account.

This action will make the account's notes unavailable while "Notes" is turned off. To access the notes from that account again, simply turn "Notes" back on.

REMOVING AN ACCOUNT

1. Open the Notes app   on your Mac.
2. In the app's menu, go to "Notes" and select "Accounts."
3. Click on the account you want to remove.
4. Click "Delete Account."

Please note that when you remove an account, the notes associated with that account will be deleted and will no longer be available on your Mac. Copies of the notes will remain on your internet account (e.g., iCloud.com or Yahoo) and any other devices where you had previously set up the account.

ADDING FILES AND IMAGES TO NOTES

1. Open the Notes app ▢ on your Mac.

2. Select the note where you want to add attachments or create a new note.

Note: If the note is locked, you must unlock it before adding attachments, tables, or links.

3. To add an attachment, do any of the following:

   a.   Add a File from the Desktop or Finder: Drag the file you want to attach into the note.

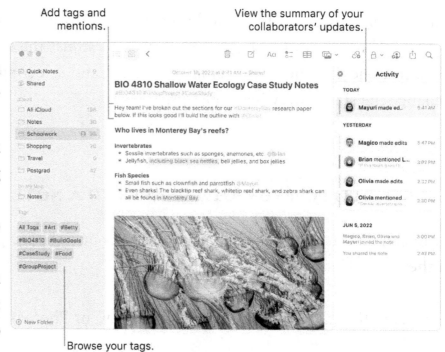

Add tags and mentions.

View the summary of your collaborators' updates.

Browse your tags.

   b.   Add a File from Your Mac: Choose "Edit" from the menu. > Select "Attach File." > Choose the file you want to attach and click "Attach."

   c.   Add a Photo from Your Photos Library: Drag a photo directly from your Photos library into the note.

Alternatively, in the Notes app, click the ▣⌄ button in the toolbar, then click "Photos," and drag a photo from the window that appears.

d. Insert a Photo or Scan from Your iPhone or iPad Camera: Click at the beginning of a line in your note > Choose "File" from the menu > Select "Insert from iPhone or iPad" > Choose to "Take Photo" or "Scan Documents" to capture a picture or scan a document with your iPhone or iPad. This will insert it into your note.

e. Insert a Sketch from Your iPhone or iPad: Click at the beginning of a line in your note > Choose "File" from the menu > Select "Insert from iPhone or iPad" > Choose "Add Sketch" to draw a sketch using your finger or Apple Pencil on your iPad. The sketch will be inserted into your note.

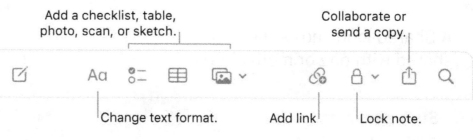

Add a checklist, table, photo, scan, or sketch.

Collaborate or send a copy.

Change text format.

Add link

Lock note.

You can change the size of all images, scanned documents, or PDFs in a note with attachments by going to "View," selecting "Attachment View," and then choosing "Set All to Small" or "Set All to Large." You can also adjust the size of individual attachments by Control-clicking them, choosing "View As," and selecting an option. Note that you can't change the size of drawings in notes.

ADDING ITEMS FROM OTHER APPS TO A NOTE

You can also attach items like map locations or webpage previews to a note directly from other apps. Here's how:

From another app (e.g., Maps, Safari, Preview, or Photos), you can do the following:

a. Share from the Toolbar: Click the "Share" button (please note that not all apps have this option) > Choose "Notes."

b. Share from a Selection: Select the text or images you want to share > Control-click your selection > Choose "Share" and then "Notes" > Click "Save" to add the item to a new note.

If you want to add an attachment to an existing note, click the "Choose Note" pop-up menu, select the name of the note, and then click "Save."

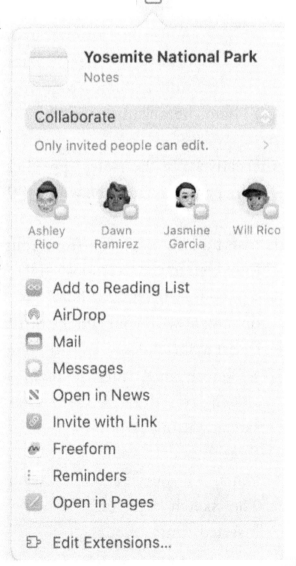

A Shared icon shows the note is shared with one or more people.

Summer Outfits
Yesterday 2 photos

PHOTOS

PHOTOS TO YOUR MAC FROM ICLOUD

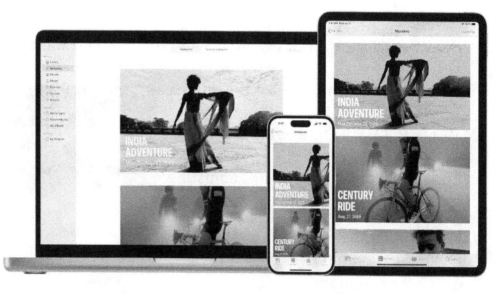

If you use iCloud, you can access your photos across all your devices by enabling iCloud Photos on your Mac, iPhone, and iPad. Go to Photos > Settings in the Photos app on your Mac, click on iCloud, and select iCloud Photos.

IMPORT PHOTOS

1. To import photos from your iPhone, iPad, or camera, connect your device or camera to your Mac, ensure it's turned on, and open Photos.
2. If you're importing from a camera, set it to download photos.
3. Click on your device or camera in the sidebar, select the photos you want to import, and then click "Import [X] Selected."

BROWSE YOUR PHOTOS

1. To view your photos by date, click "Library" in the sidebar. You can then select "Years," "Months," or "Days" in the toolbar.
2. Click "All Photos" to see your entire collection.
3. To view photos of specific people or those taken in specific locations, click "People" or "Places" in the sidebar.

CROP AND STRAIGHTEN PHOTOS

1. You can crop photos to remove unwanted areas or straighten photos taken at an angle.
2. Double-click on a photo, click "Edit" in the toolbar, and then

select "Crop."

3. Drag the selection rectangle to enclose the area you want to keep and use the

"Straighten" slider to adjust the photo's a

IMPROVE THE LOOK OF PHOTOS

1. Enhance your photos by adjusting brightness, color, and more.
2. Double-click on a photo, click "Edit" in the toolbar, and choose the "Light" or "Colour" options.
3. Drag the slider to achieve the desired look, or use the "Auto" option to let Photos make automatic adjustments.

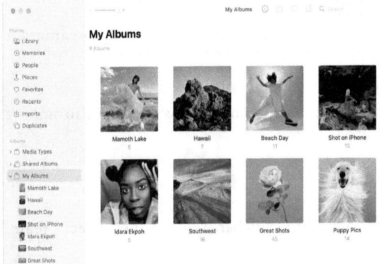

ORGANIZE PHOTOS IN ALBUMS

1. To organize your photos, create albums as you like.
2. Go to "File" > "New Album," provide a name for the album, and press Return.
3. To add photos to the album, click "Library" in the sidebar, and then drag photos to the new album in
4. the sidebar.

To optimize storage in the Photos app 🌸 on your Mac when using iCloud Photos, follow these steps:

1. Open the Photos app 🌸 on your Mac.
2. In the menu bar at the top of your screen,

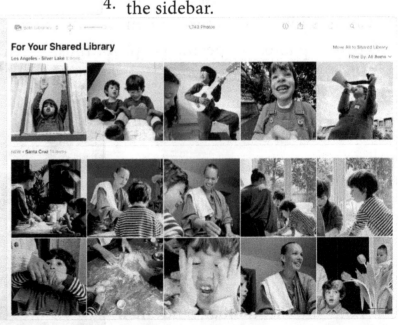

click "Photos."

3. Select "Preferences."then in the Preferences window, click on the "iCloud" tab.

4. Ensure that the "iCloud Photos" checkbox is selected. This enables iCloud Photos, which is required for optimizing Mac storage.

5. Below the checkbox, you'll find an option called "Optimise Mac Storage." Select this option.

6. Once you've selected "Optimise Mac Storage," your Mac will store smaller versions of your photos locally when storage space is limited, while keeping the original, full-size photos in iCloud. This helps free up space on your Mac.

TO RESTORE THE ORIGINAL, FULL-SIZE PHOTOS TO YOUR MAC, FOLLOW THESE STEPS

1. In the Photos app 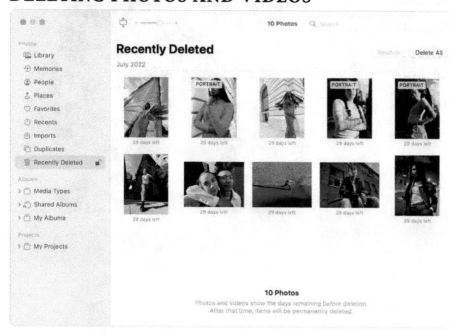 on your Mac, go to the menu bar and click "Photos."
2. Select "Preferences" to open the Preferences window.
3. Click on the "iCloud" tab.
4. Locate the "Optimise Mac Storage" option, and this time, unselect it.
5. After you've turned off the optimization feature, the Photos app will begin downloading the original, full-size photos to your Mac. Be patient, as this process might take some time depending on the number and size of your photos.

By following these steps, you can optimize storage in the Photos app on your Mac and easily manage your photo library while conserving local storage space.

DELETING PHOTOS AND VIDEOS

1. Open the Photos app on your Mac.
2. Choose the items (photos or videos) that you want to delete by clicking on them in your library.
3. To delete the selected items and move them to the "Recently Deleted" album, you can either:

• Press the Delete key if you're

in "Days" view, and then click the Delete button that appears.

- Press Delete to remove items from an album, but they'll remain in your library.
- To permanently delete items from the "Recently Deleted" album, press Command-Delete, then open the "Recently Deleted" album.

RESTORING RECENTLY DELETED ITEMS

1. In the Photos app 🌸 , you can find the "Recently Deleted" album in the sidebar. Click on it to access recently deleted items.
2. If the "Recently Deleted" album is locked, you can unlock it either by using Touch ID or by entering your password.
3. Select the items that you want to restore to your Photos library.
4. Click the "Recover" button to restore the selected items.

If you use iCloud Photos, you can recover photos and videos from iCloud within 30 days of deletion. If you don't use iCloud Photos, deleted items will be removed from your Mac only.

In addition, if you've set up Time Machine to back up your Mac, you may be able to recover items that have been permanently deleted from your Mac or iCloud using your backups. You can refer to the "Restore a Photos library from Time Machine" feature for this purpose.

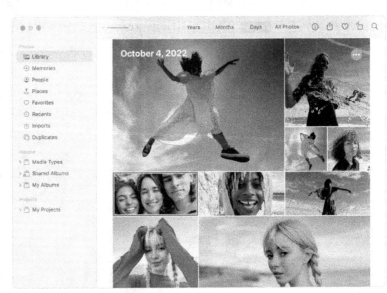

ICLOUD

Using iCloud Photos on your Mac is a convenient way to store and access your photos and videos across multiple devices.

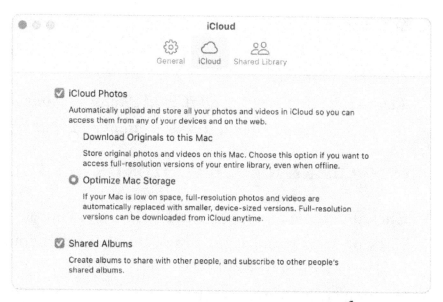

BEFORE YOU BEGIN

1. Ensure that your Mac and other devices have the latest software updates.

2. Sign in with your Apple ID. If you're not signed in, go to Apple menu > System Preferences, then click "Sign in with your Apple ID" and follow the prompts.

TO TURN ON ICLOUD PHOTOS

1. Open the Photos app on your Mac.
2. Click on "Photos" in the top menu bar, then select "Preferences."
3. In the Preferences window, click on the "iCloud" tab.
4. Check the "iCloud Photos" option to enable it.
5. You'll have two options:

    • "Download Originals to this Mac": This option stores the full-size versions of your photos both on your Mac and in iCloud.

    • "Optimise Mac Storage": This option stores smaller versions of your photos on your Mac when storage space is limited. It keeps the original, full-size photos in iCloud. Choose this option to save space on your Mac. You can always restore the originals to your Mac by selecting "Download Originals to this Mac."

6. Once you've selected your preference, iCloud Photos will start syncing your photos to iCloud. This initial upload may take some time, but you can continue using Photos during this process.

TO TURN OFF ICLOUD PHOTOS ON YOUR MAC

1. Open the Photos app on your Mac.
2. Click on "Photos" in the top menu bar, then select "Preferences."
3. In the Preferences window, click on the "iCloud" tab.
4. Uncheck the "iCloud Photos" option to disable it.

5. You can choose to download photos and videos from iCloud to your Mac by clicking "Download" or remove photos and videos that haven't been fully downloaded by clicking "Remove."

Please note that turning off iCloud Photos on your Mac doesn't delete your photos from iCloud. They'll still be available to your other devices that use iCloud Photos.

TO STOP USING ICLOUD PHOTOS ON ALL YOUR APPLE DEVICES

1. Click the Apple menu ![Apple icon] on your Mac and choose "System Preferences."
2. Click on your name at the top of the sidebar. If your name isn't visible, you may need to sign in with your Apple ID.
3. Click on "iCloud" on the right.
4. Click "Manage," then select "Photos." and then tap "Turn Off and Delete."

Warning: If you turn off iCloud Photos on all your devices, your photos and videos will be deleted from iCloud after 30 days. Be sure to click "Undo Delete" within that time frame if you want to recover them.

VIEWING MEMORIES & HOW TO PLAY A MEMORY

1. Open the Photos app ![Photos icon] on your Mac and tap "Memories" in the sidebar.
2. Scroll through the various memories.
3. Double-click the memory you want to play.
4. While the memory is playing, you can start or stop it by clicking the Play button or pressing the Spacebar. You can also navigate through individual photos in the memory by using the arrow keys or trackpad swipes. To display memory photos in a grid, click the "Grid View" button. You can exit a memory by clicking the left arrow in the toolbar.

HOW TO CREATE YOUR OWN MEMORY FROM AN ALBUM

1. Select an album in the sidebar.
2. Click "Play Memory Video" from the toolbar.
3. If you want to add the new memory to your Memories collection, click the "Favourite" button. If you change your mind, you can click the "Favourite" button again to remove it as a favorite.

HOW TO SHARE A MEMORY

1. Click "Memories" in the sidebar.
2. Find and double-click the memory you want to share.
3. Press the Spacebar to stop playing the memory, then the "Share" button in the toolbar.
4. Choose how you want to share the memory, whether it's through Messages, Mail, or AirDrop.

HOW TO SHARE PHOTOS FROM A MEMORY

1. Click "Memories" in the sidebar.
2. Find and double-click the memory containing the photos you want to share.
3. Press the Spacebar to stop playing the memory then click the "Grid View" button.
4. Select the photos you want to share and click the "Share" button in the toolbar.
5. Choose your preferred sharing method, like Messages, Mail, or AirDrop.

HOW TO ADD A MEMORY AS A FAVORITE

1. Click "Memories" in the sidebar.
2. Scroll to the memory you want to make a favorite.
3. Click the "Favourite" button on the memory. You can also do this while viewing the memory.
4. To access your favorite memories, click "Favourite Memories" in the toolbar.

Automatically create a personalized video of special moments.

View your photos by Years, Months, Days, or All Photos.

PODCASTS

Do you want to explore, subscribe to, and enjoy your favorite podcasts on your Mac? Then Apple Podcasts is the perfect platform for you!

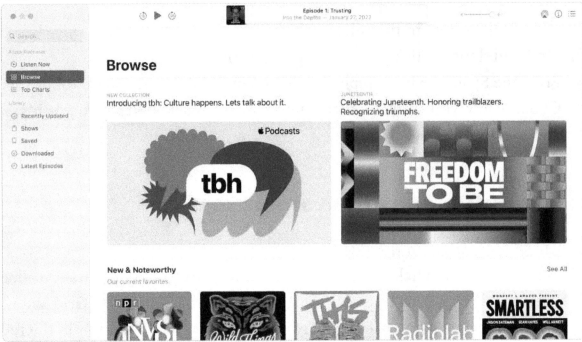

Here's a guide to help you get started with Apple Podcasts and make the most of its features:

- Listen Now: This is where you can start exploring your subscribed podcasts, and also find personalized recommendations for new podcasts based on your interests. It's your one-stop-shop for all your listening needs. You can even use Siri to interact with your podcasts and pick up where you last left off.

DISCOVER NEW PODCASTS

- Use the "Listen Now" section to discover new and interesting podcasts based on topics or shows you enjoy. If you find a show you like, you can subscribe to it or add an episode to your library for later. You'll also get suggestions for similar topics and shows based on what you enjoy. Check out the "Top Charts" to see which podcasts are currently trending.

SHARED WITH YOU

- If your friends share podcasts with you in Messages, those episodes will appear in the "Shared with You" section of Listen Now.

SAVE EPISODES TO YOUR LIBRARY

- You can save individual episodes to your library by clicking the "Add" button ➕ . To keep up with all new episodes for a podcast, click "Subscribe." If you want to listen offline, click the "Download" button ☁.

SEARCH BY HOST OR GUEST

- When you search for a specific topic or person, you can see results for shows they host, shows where they're a guest, and even shows where they're mentioned or discussed.

FOLLOW YOUR FAVORITES

- Click "Follow" to add a show to your favorites. This way, you'll never miss a new episode. You can easily see what's new in the "Recently Updated" section of your library.

SAVE IDEAS WITH QUICK NOTE

- If you come across a podcast you want to remember for later, you can create a Quick Note. This helps you save the information, and you can find it later in the sidebar of the Notes app. To create a Quick Note, press Fn-Q or use a specified Hot Corner.

USE AIRPLAY

- You can use AirPlay to play a podcast through an external speaker. Click the Control Center icon in the menu bar, then click Screen Mirroring to select an available speaker.

With Apple Podcasts, you can enjoy a wide range of podcasts, discover new content, and keep up with your favorite shows. It's a great way to stay informed and entertained while using your Mac.

PREVIEW

As a Mac user, you can take advantage of the Preview app to view and edit PDFs and images, fill out and sign forms online, annotate PDFs, convert graphic file types, password protect PDFs, highlight and translate text, and more.

View and Edit PDFs and Images: You can easily open and view PDF and image files using Preview, and make simple edits to these documents.

Fill in PDF Forms: Interactive PDF forms can be filled in by clicking on form fields and typing your text directly into them.

Password Protect PDFs: To secure a PDF, you can assign a password that users must enter before they can view the contents, which is ideal for protecting sensitive information.

Add and Remove PDF Pages: You can manipulate the pages in a PDF by adding, deleting, or rearranging them, making it easy to customize a PDF document.

Copy Pages from One PDF to Another: Preview allows you to copy pages from one PDF and paste them into another, which is handy when you need to combine content from multiple PDFs.

Translate Text: You can highlight text in a PDF, right-click, and select the "Translate" option to get a translation. Plus, you can download languages for offline use.

View and Convert Image Files: Preview can open and convert images to various file types, including JPEG, PDF, PNG, TIFF, and more. This feature is helpful for converting and saving images in different formats.

REMINDERS

The Reminders app ⦚ on your Mac is a useful tool for keeping track of tasks and to-dos. To make the most of the app, here are some key features and tips you can use:

Tags: You can add tags to your reminders to help organize them. By clicking on one or more tags in the sidebar, you can quickly filter reminders based on those tags.

Custom Smart Lists: Smart Lists automatically sort your upcoming reminders based on criteria like dates, times, tags, locations, flags, or priority. To create your own Custom Smart Lists, simply add filters to suit your specific needs.

Save Lists as Templates: If you have a list that you want to reuse in the future, you can save it as a template. Simply select the list in the sidebar, then choose "File > Save as Template."

Today and Scheduled Lists: The Today and Scheduled lists in the sidebar group reminders based on their due dates and times. This helps you keep track of what's coming up and ensures you don't miss any important tasks.

Smart Suggestions: Reminders can automatically suggest dates, times, and locations for a reminder based on your past reminders. This feature can save you time when creating new reminders.

Collaboration: You can collaborate with others on a list by sending invitations through Messages or Mail, or by sharing a link. Click the Share button ⬆, then choose how to share the list. Once others are invited, you can track activity and manage collaboration using the Collaborate button ⊚.

Assign Responsibility: When sharing a list, you can assign reminders to specific people, ensuring that they receive notifications. This is useful for dividing tasks and clarifying responsibilities.

Subtasks and Groups: You can create subtasks by pressing Command-] or dragging one reminder on top of another. Subtasks are indented under their parent reminders. You can also organize your lists by creating groups. To create a group, choose "File > New Group."

Completed Smart List: The Completed Smart List in the sidebar allows you to review all your finished reminders, including their completion dates.

Reminder Suggestions in Mail: When using Mail, Siri can recognize potential reminders and make suggestions for creating them. This feature can be especially helpful during email correspondence.

Adding Reminders Quickly: You can add reminders quickly using natural language. For instance, you can type "Take Amy to soccer every Wednesday at 5 PM" to create a repeating reminder for that specific day and time.

By using these features and tips, you can stay organized with your tasks and to-dos and make the most of the Reminders app on your Mac.

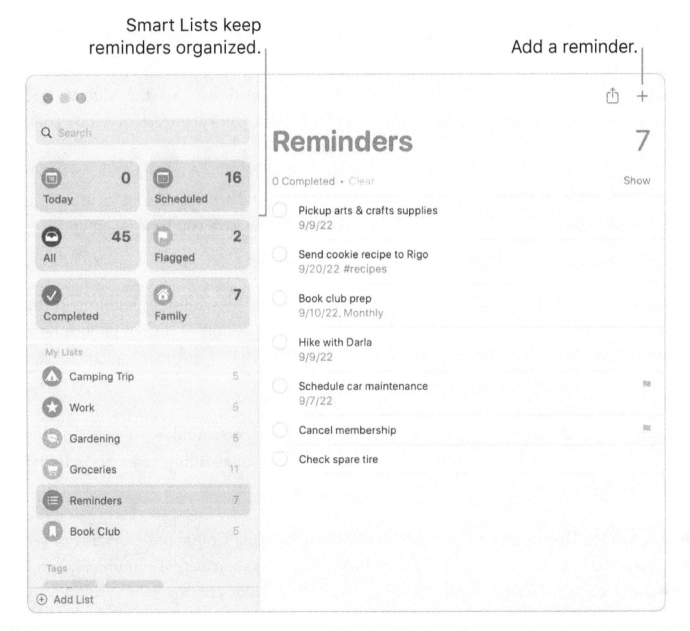

SAFARI

If you're using a Mac, Safari is a great browser to use for browsing the internet and finding information. Here's how to get started with Safari:

1. **Search for Information:** You can use the Smart Search field at the top of the Safari window to search the web for almost anything. Simply type in what you're looking for, such as "ice-cream near me," and then click on one of the suggested search results that appear.

Type what you're looking for.

2. **Go to a Website:** The Smart Search field also allows you to visit a specific website. Simply enter the website's name or web address, and Safari will take you there.

3. **Choose a Homepage:** If you frequently visit a particular website and want it to appear every time you open a new Safari window, you can set it as your homepage. To do this, go to Safari > Preferences, click on General, and then enter the web page address. Alternatively, you can click "Set to Current Page" to set the web page you're currently viewing as your homepage.

4. **Bookmark Websites:** When you come across websites you'd like to revisit, you can bookmark them for easy access. Click the Share button in the toolbar and choose "Add Bookmark." To access bookmarked websites, click the Sidebar button in the toolbar, then click the Bookmarks button .

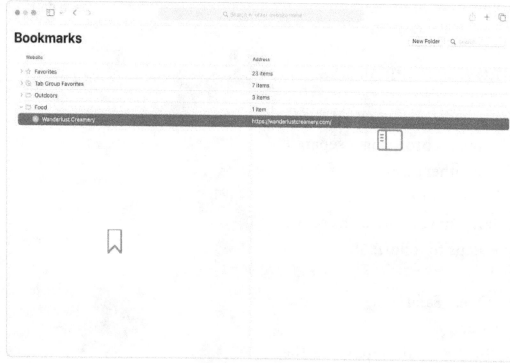

WEBSITE INTO AN APP

You can convert a website to be like an app on your Mac using Safari!

Here's a step-by-step guide to help you:

1. Open Safari  on your Mac.
2. Visit the website that you want to convert into an app.
3. Click the Share button located in the toolbar, which looks like a square with an arrow pointing upwards.
4. From the Share menu, select "Add to Dock."
5. Click "Add" to confirm.

The web app has its own menus in the menu bar.

An icon for the web app is added to the Dock.

After completing the above steps, the web app will be added to your Dock and Launchpad. If you were previously signed in to the website, you'll likely be automatically signed in to the web app. Your username and password will remain the same.

The web app will have a simplified toolbar and you'll receive notifications from it, just like in any other app. This allows you to easily access your favorite websites as standalone applications.

BROWSING PROFILES

If you want to keep your personal browsing separate from other aspects of your life, you can create a profile in Safari on your Mac. Here are the steps to follow:

1. Open Safari 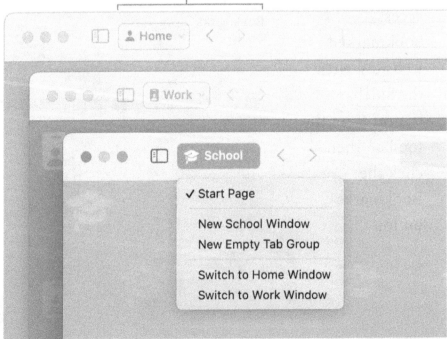 on your Mac.
2. In the Safari app, go to the

Create a profile for each part of your life.

menu and choose "Safari" located at the top left corner of the screen.

3. From the Safari menu, select "Settings," then click on "Profiles."

4. If you haven't used profiles before, you'll be prompted to "Start Using Profiles." Click on it to begin setting up your profiles.

5. Next, click the "Add" button ╼ below the profiles list to create a new profile.

6. Enter a name for this profile. You can also choose an icon and color to make it easily identifiable.

7. Select a bookmarks folder for your favorite websites to be associated with this profile.

8. Click "Create Profile" to finish the setup.

9. If you have browser extensions, you can click on "Extensions" to select the ones you want to use with this profile.

10. Keep in mind that if you store passwords in iCloud Keychain, they will be available in any profile you create.

It's important to note that, in addition to any profiles you create, you always have a "Personal (Default)" profile. You can change the name, icon, and color of your personal profile as well. This way, you can keep your browsing organized and separate for different aspects of your life.

LOCK PRIVATE BROWSING WINDOWS

Here's how to lock private browsing windows in Safari on your Mac and require your password or Touch ID to unlock them:

1. Open Safari 🧭 on your Mac.
2. Go to the Safari menu in the top left corner of the screen and select "Settings."
3. Click on "Privacy."
4. Under Privacy settings, select "Require password to view locked tabs." If you have a Mac or Apple keyboard with Touch ID, you can also choose "Require Touch ID to view locked tabs." Choose the option that best suits you.

Private Browsing Is Locked

Touch ID or enter the password for the user "Danny Rico" to view locked tabs.

Enter password

5. Once you've chosen the desired option, your private browsing windows will be locked automatically under certain conditions, but you can also manually lock them.

To manually lock private browsing windows:

Go to the Safari menu and select "Window." > Choose "Lock All Private Windows."

This will immediately lock all your private browsing windows, and they will require your password or Touch ID to unlock.

Keep in mind that private browsing windows will also lock automatically under the following conditions:

- When you lock your screen.

- When a password is required after the screen saver starts.

- When a password is required after the display is turned off.

- When you minimize the windows and leave them inactive for a period of time.

- When you leave the windows open in the background but don't interact with them for a period of time.

If you ever want to allow private browsing windows to remain unlocked, you can go back to the Privacy settings in Safari and unselect the "Require password to view locked tabs" or "Require Touch ID to view locked tabs" option, depending on your preference.

ALLOW OR BLOCK POP-UPS ON ALL WEBSITES

1. Open Safari on your Mac.
2. Click on Safari in the menu bar, then select "Settings."
3. Choose "Websites."
4. Click "Pop-up Windows" on the left. If you don't see "Pop-up Windows," make sure you scroll to the bottom of the list.
5. If there are websites listed below "Configured Websites," and you want to change the settings for these sites (for example, changing from Allow to Block), select each website, then click "Remove."
6. If you don't see "Configured Websites," it means you haven't set pop-up blocking for any sites yet or you've cleared the list.
7. Click the "When visiting other websites" pop-up menu, then choose one of the following:

- Allow: Pop-ups for all websites will appear.
- Block and Notify: Pop-ups for all websites won't appear, but you'll be notified when a

Click to show the blocked pop-up windows.

Show blocked pop-up window

127

pop-up is blocked, and you can choos show it by clicking the "Show" button   in the Smart Search field.

- Block: Pop-ups for all websites won't appear.

Remember that blocking pop-ups may also prevent some content you want to see. If you continue to see pop-ups on a website that you've set to block, it could be due to unwanted software on your Mac, and you might need to address that separately.

GOT COOKIES??

If you want to clear cookies in Safari on your Mac, follow these easy steps:

1. Open Safari ◈ on your Mac.
2. Click on "Safari" in the menu bar located at the top left corner of your screen.
3. From the drop-down menu, select "Preferences."
4. In the Preferences window, choose "Privacy" from the toolbar.
5. Under the "Privacy" tab, you will see an option labeled "Manage Website Data." Click on it.
6. A new window will appear, displaying a list of all websites that have stored cookies and website data on your Mac.
7. To remove data from a specific website, select the website from the list.
8. Click on the "Remove" button to remove data for the selected website.
9. If you want to remove data for all websites, click on the "Remove All" button.

Please keep in mind that deleting cookies and website data may affect your experience on certain websites, such as logging you out or altering website behavior. Furthermore, removing cookies in Safari may also affect cookies in other apps.

BROWSE PRIVATELY

If you want to browse the internet privately on your Mac, you can follow these steps:

1. First, open Safari ◈ on your Mac.
2. Next, click on "File" in the Safari menu at the top left of your screen.
3. Then, select "New Private Window".

128

4. A new window will open with a dark Smart Search field, indicating that you are browsing privately.

5. When you use Private Browsing, the following happens:

- Browsing in one tab is isolated from browsing in other tabs, preventing websites from tracking your activity across multiple sessions.

- Webpages you visit and your AutoFill information aren't saved.

- Your open web pages aren't stored in iCloud, so they won't appear on other Apple devices.

- Your recent searches aren't included in the Smart Search field's results list.

- Items you download aren't included in the downloads list (but remain on your computer).

- Changes to cookies and website data aren't saved.

6. To always browse privately, you can go to Safari 🧭 > Settings > General and choose "A new private window" under "Safari opens with."

7. To stop browsing privately, close the private window, switch to a non-private Safari window, or open a new non-private window using File > New Window.

Remember that when you browse privately, your browsing history and website data won't be saved, providing you with enhanced privacy during your online activities.

STOCKS

The Stocks app 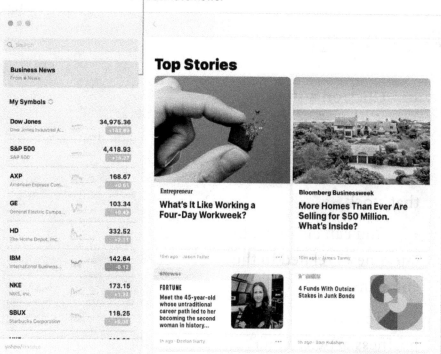 on your Mac is a useful tool for keeping track of financial markets and your investments.

Below are the key features and how to use them:

CREATE AND

CUSTOMIZE

WATCHLISTS

- To create a new watchlist, click on "My Symbols" and then select "New Watchlist."

- Add stocks to your watchlist by entering a company name or stock symbol in the search field.

- Double-click the stock symbol in the search results to view detailed stock information.

- To add a stock to a watchlist, click the "Add" button + in the top-right corner and choose the watchlist you want to add it to.

- To remove a stock from a watchlist, Control-click the stock symbol and select "Manage Symbol." Then, deselect the checkbox next to the watchlist you want to remove it from.

- Control-clicking a stock in your watchlist will allow you to open it in a new tab or window.

MONITOR MARKET CHANGES

- In your watchlist, you can view real-time market data.

- You can switch between price change, percentage change, and market capitalization by clicking on the green or red button below each price.

- Color-coded sparklines provide a visual representation of the stock's performance throughout the day.

READ ARTICLES

- Click on a stock in your watchlist to access an interactive chart and additional details about that stock.

- You can also read the latest news related to the company.

- To access curated business articles from Apple News, click "Business News" at the top of your watchlist.

Click to cycle between price change, percentage change, and market capitalization.

GET A DEEPER VIEW

- The Stocks app allows you to explore historical data. You can switch between different timeframes (e.g., last week, last month, or last year) by clicking the buttons above the chart.

SYNC WATCHLISTS ACROSS DEVICES

- Signing in with the same Apple ID on multiple devices ensures your watchlist remains consistent across all of them, providing you access to the same information on all your Apple devices.

Please note that Apple News stories and Top Stories are available in the U.S., Canada, the UK, and Australia, while news stories in other countries and regions are provided by Yahoo.

APPLE TV

The Apple TV app on your Mac is the hub for all your TV and streaming content. It offers a range of features that make it easy for you to access your favorite content.

Here's what you can do with the Apple TV app:

1. **Apple TV+:** Subscribe to and watch Apple TV+, Apple's streaming service featuring original TV shows and movies created by some of the most creative people in the entertainment industry. Note that the availability of Apple TV+ varies by country and region.

2. **MLS Season Pass:** If you're a fan of Major League Soccer (MLS), you can subscribe to MLS Season Pass in the Apple TV app. This provides access to all MLS regular season and playoff matches and hundreds of MLS NEXT Pro and MLS NEXT games. Note that the availability of MLS Season Pass may differ depending on your location.

3. **Apple TV Channels:** You can subscribe to various Apple TV channels, such as Paramount+ and STARZ, to access additional content. The availability of Apple TV channels may differ by country and region.

4. **Personalized Recommendations:** The app offers content recommendations based on your viewing history and preferences, making it easier to discover new shows and movies you might enjoy.

5. **Content Sharing:** You can watch movies and shows shared with you from the Messages app.

6. **Watch Together with SharePlay:** The Apple TV app integrates with SharePlay and the FaceTime app, allowing you to watch content with friends and family, even if you're not in the same location.

7. **Access the Store:** You can access the Apple TV Store to purchase, rent, or subscribe to

the world's best movies and TV shows, including Apple TV channels that you haven't subscribed to yet.

8. **Manage Your Collection:** The app provides access to your entire movie and TV show collection, making it easy to organize and access your media.

Keep in mind that the availability of some features, such as Apple TV+ and MLS Season Pass, may vary by country or region. This means that the content and subscriptions available to you in the Apple TV app could differ based on your location.

SIGN IN TO START WATCHING NOW

To buy, rent, or subscribe to content on Apple TV app using your Mac, you need to sign in with your Apple ID. Here's how you can sign in or create a new Apple ID if you don't have one yet:

CREATING A NEW APPLE ID

1. Open the Apple TV app  on your Mac.
2. Click on "Account" in the menu bar at the top of the screen.
3. Choose "Sign In."
4. Click on "Create New Apple ID."
5. Follow the on-screen instructions to set up a new Apple ID.

Please note that PayPal is available as a payment method in some regions. However, it may not be accepted in all countries.

SIGNING IN OR OUT OF THE APPLE TV APP

Once you have an Apple ID, you can use it to sign in or out of the Apple TV app. Here's how:

1. In the Apple TV app on your Mac, click on "Account" in the menu bar.
2. Select either "Sign In" or "Sign Out," depending on your current status.

133

3. If you can't remember your Apple ID or password, click on "Forgot Apple ID or Password?" and follow the instructions to recover your credentials.

We recommend signing out of the app if you share your computer with others to prevent unauthorized purchases using your account.

By signing in, you can easily access your account information, purchase history, and enjoy a seamless experience when renting or buying movies and TV shows through the Apple TV app

WATCH TOGETHER

Watching movies or TV shows with your friends or family can be a fun activity, especially when you are not together physically. With SharePlay in the Apple TV app, you can enjoy synchronized viewing while on a FaceTime call.

WATCH TOGETHER WITH SHAREPLAY

1. Open the FaceTime app on your Mac and start or answer a call.
2. Open the Apple TV app on your Mac or another caller's device and start watching a movie or show.
3. If prompted, click "View" to open the TV app on your Mac and then click "Join."

The video will start playing in sync on all devices participating in the FaceTime call. Each person can control the playback using their respective devices while the FaceTime app window remains open.

To modify the SharePlay settings, you can click the SharePlay button in the macOS menu bar.

LEAVING THE CALL OR SHARED VIEWING SESSION

Anyone can leave the FaceTime call while continuing the shared viewing session or leave both. Here is how you can do it:

1. While using SharePlay in the Apple TV app  on your Mac, click the SharePlay button in the macOS menu bar.
2. Click the "Leave Call" button.
3. Choose to either "Continue" or "Leave SharePlay."

Click to turn off your camera.
Click to mute your microphone.
Click to open Messages.
Click to leave the call.

If you initiated the shared session and choose "Leave SharePlay," the shared session will end for everyone.

START A TEXT CONVERSATION

During a SharePlay watch session in the Apple TV app on your Mac, you can initiate a text conversation in Messages with all the participants:

1. Click the SharePlay button in the macOS menu bar.
2. Click the "Messages" button.
3. The Messages app will open, allowing you to enter your messages in the text field.

ADD VIDEO EFFECTS

While watching with SharePlay, you can add video effects and animated reactions to your live video in the FaceTime app window (requires macOS 12 or later and Apple silicon):

1. Click the SharePlay button ⬚ in the macOS menu bar.
2. Click the disclosure arrow to the right of "FaceTime HD Camera."
3. Choose video effects such as Portrait, Studio Light, or Reactions (animated effects created using hand gestures).

ADJUST MICROPHONE SENSITIVITY

You can adjust the sensitivity of your microphone to isolate your voice or capture surrounding sounds (requires macOS 12 or later and Apple silicon):

1. Click the SharePlay button ⬚ in the macOS menu bar.
2. Click the disclosure triangle to the right of "Mic Mode."
3. Select a microphone option: Standard, Voice Isolation, or Wide Spectrum.

USE AIRPLAY

If you want to share what you're watching during SharePlay with an Apple TV on the same network:

1. While using SharePlay in the Apple TV app ⬚ on your Mac, move your pointer over the viewer window to show playback controls.
2. Click the AirPlay button ⬚ and choose the Apple TV you want to use for watching.

Please note that SharePlay may not be available in all countries or regions, and the availability of specific content and features may vary.

VOICE MEMOS

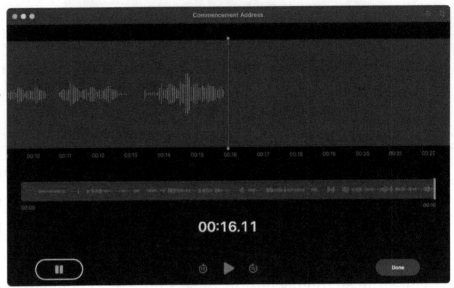

Recording audio on your MacBook becomes easy with the help of Voice Memos. Let's take a look at some of the major features and actions that you can perform with Voice Memos:

RECORDING

1. To start recording, click on the Record button ⬤ .
2. Click Done when you are finished with recording.
3. You can rename your recording by clicking on the default name and entering a new one for better identification.
4. To play back a recording, click on the Play button ▶.

ACCESS ON ALL DEVICES

When you sign in using the same Apple ID, your voice memos become available on all your devices. This means that you can access recordings made with your iPhone or iPad right from your Mac.

ORGANIZE WITH FOLDERS

1. Create folders to keep your Voice Memos organized. Click on the Sidebar button, then the New Folder button at the bottom of the sidebar.
2. Enter a name for the folder and click Save.
3. To add a recording to the folder, press and hold the Option key while dragging the recording to the folder.

MARK AS FAVORITE

1. You can mark a recording as a favorite for quick access later.
2. Select a recording, then click the Favorite button ♡ in the toolbar.
3. Click the Sidebar button ⊞ to see all your favorites.

Mark recordings as Favorites.

Create new folders to organize your recordings.

SKIP SILENCE

1. Skip over gaps or silent portions in your audio.
2. Click the Playback Settings button at the top of the Voice Memos window and turn on "Skip Silence."

CHANGE PLAYBACK SPEED

1. Speed up or slow down the playback speed of your audio.
2. Click the Playback Settings button at the top of the Voice Memos window.
3. Drag the slider left or right to adjust the speed.

ENHANCE A RECORDING

1. Improve the sound quality of your Voice Memos by reducing background noise and room reverberation.
2. Click the Playback Settings button at the top of the Voice Memos window and turn on "Enhance Recording."

These features allow you to record, manage, and enhance your audio recordings with Voice Memos on your MacBook.

Dear Apple Pro!
I hope you have enjoyed exploring the world of Apple devices. Your feedback means a lot to me and it can be a valuable gift to fellow readers who are considering this guide. Writing a review on Amazon is a simple yet incredibly helpful way

to pay it forward(Do not worry, its free!). Scan this QR code to take you straight there!

Your words have the power to inspire confidence in others, just as I've aimed to do with this book. Whether you found the content insightful, the instructions clear, or if you have any suggestions for improvement (I WILL incorporate it into following books), your review will be appreciated.

By sharing your thoughts, you not only assist other seniors in making an informed choice but also support the author (that's me!). Your review provides insights that can guide prospective readers, making their journey with the Apple products more enjoyable and stress-free. If you made it this far, I am offering the digital beta copy of our next book for all customers that volunteer to leave a review and email me a picture of their review posted on Amazon!
Email me at:
JasonBrownPublishing@gmail.com

Thank you for considering this request. Your words can make a big difference, and together, we can make the Apple world even more accessible and enjoyable for everyone, everywhere!

Thank you,
Jason Brown

COMPANION GUIDES!

If you found our "Macbook for Seniors: A Simple Step-by-Step Guide" helpful, then you'll definitely want to check out our companion guides "iPhone for Seniors - A Simple Step by Step Guide for Beginners" & "Apple Watch for Seniors: A Simple Step by Step Guide"

These guides will help you navigate your Apple products with ease, from sending messages to capturing memories and everything in between. They are specifically designed to make technology accessible for beginners & seniors to confidently dive into the world of technology!

Are you ready to unlock more possibilities?
Scan these QR codes on your iPhone and get your copies!

www.ingramcontent.com/pod-product-compliance
Lightning Source LLC
Chambersburg PA
CBHW080536060326
40690CB00022B/5147